An Enduring Legacy

The Basque Series

JOHN BIETER & MARK BIETER

An Enduring Legacy

The Story of Basques in Idaho

UNIVERSITY OF NEVADA PRESS ▲▲ RENO & LAS VEGAS

The Basque Series
Series Editor: William A. Douglass

University of Nevada Press, Reno, Nevada 89557 USA
Copyright © 2000 by University of Nevada Press
All rights reserved
Manufactured in the United States of America
Designer: Carrie House

Library of Congress Cataloging-in-Publication Data
Bieter, John, 1962–
    An enduring legacy : the story of Basques in Idaho / John
Bieter and Mark Bieter.
       p.   cm. — (The Basque series)
Includes bibliographical references and index.
    ISBN 0-87417-333-7
    1. Basque Americans—Idaho—History.   2. Immigrants—
Idaho—History.   3. Idaho—Ethnic relations.   I. Bieter,
Mark, 1967–   II. Title.   III. Series
    F755.B15 B48 2000
    979.6004'9992—dc21
00-008233

Frontispiece: Basque picnic, Mode Country Club, Boise, Idaho,
summer, 1934. Photo courtesy Basque Museum and Cultural
Center, Boise, Idaho.

The majority of photographs in this book credited to the Basque
Museum and Cultural Center are from the Juanita Uberuaga
Hormaechea Collection.

The paper used in this book meets the requirements
of American National Standard for Information
Sciences—Permanence of Paper for Printed Library
Materials, ANSI Z39.48-1984. Binding materials were
selected for strength and durability.

University of Nevada Press Paperback Edition, 2004
First Printing

13 12 11 10 09 08 07 06 05 04   5 4 3 2 1
ISBN   0-87417-568-2   (pbk.)

In loving memory of Mom and Dad

CONTENTS

ILLUSTRATIONS

ACKNOWLEDGMENTS

Books almost always involve the help and advice of many people, and this effort, our first, was certainly no exception. Since we began this project in 1990, we have benefited from the generosity of dozens of individuals and organizations. We would like to acknowledge the Basque Government, the Idaho Humanities Council, and the University of Nevada, Reno, for their financial support in the research and writing of the manuscript. Many thanks are due to Mary K. Aucutt and Helen Berria, who helped us throughout the project, especially when many thought it could not be completed. We also thank Julio Bilbao, Justo Sarria, Bob Sims, and Tim Woodward, who served on an advisory committee for our grants; Todd Shallat, Milt Small, and Hugh Lovin, whose advice and inspiration at the beginning proved invaluable; David Ensunsa, for his research during the early stages; William A. Douglass and the staff of the Basque Studies Program, for their support for our research in Reno; Sara Vélez Mallea and Jan McInroy, who helped shape the finished product; the Basque Museum and Cultural Center, for giving us a quiet place to write and research; Dave Lachiondo, for edits on our first drafts; Virginia Garmendia, for locating important documents during our research in the Basque Country; our siblings, for listening to us for hours; to Shannon Bieter, for her care and patience; Pam Burns and Darlyne Pape, for general encouragement and edits; Al Erquiaga, for special help with research on the Oinkaris; and most especially to all of those we interviewed, for giving us so many wonderful stories and remembrances. We also give special thanks to the

Bilbao family, who were so generous with their time and the sharing of their experiences, and Patty Miller at the Basque Museum & Cultural Center, who helped us with just about everything.

Finally, we would like to acknowledge those we relied on who, sadly, did not live to see the publication of this book. We remember especially Joe Eiguren, Jay Hormachea, and our parents, Pat and Eloise Bieter. We hope this book in some small way helps honor all the things they worked so hard for during their wonderful lives.

An Enduring Legacy

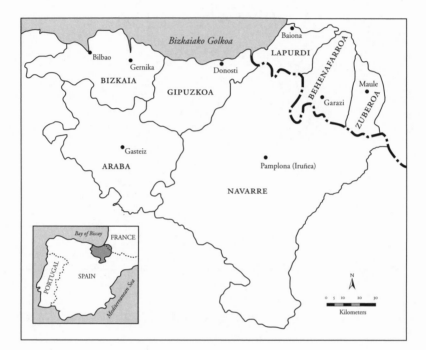

The Basque Country. (Map by Cameron Sutherland)

Introduction

They sat in the Nevada desert, thirsty after a full day without water, afraid they would not survive the choice they had made.

It was late spring of 1889. José Navarro and Antonio Azcuenaga, two men in their early twenties from the Basque province of Bizkaia, had gained some success after several years of hard labor in northwestern Nevada. They had heard rumors of better opportunities in Oregon and Idaho, however, and decided to move. They invested in a horse to carry provisions and set out on the trek north across the desert.

The area was dusty and crackly dry, a world away from the green hills rising above the ocean in the Basque Country. Despite having been in the West for some time, Navarro and Azcuenaga did not know what to expect on this journey north, and they suffered the consequences of poor planning. On the first day they managed only twelve miles, and by the end of the second they had all but exhausted their water supply. They stopped and considered their options. Not knowing how many miles of desert remained before them, they realized that it seemed foolish to continue north. But without water, it was equally inconceivable to turn back and retrace their steps. They decided to press on. Two days later they finally reached the Owyhee River, plunged in, and drank as much water as their stomachs could hold.

Several days later they ran out of water again. They decided to unload their supplies and clothing from the horse, and Navarro rode away in search of water, while Azcuenaga remained in the desert with the supplies. Navarro found a creek and returned for Azcuenaga, who by this time was nearly dead from thirst. Navarro lifted him onto the horse and, leaving most of their clothing and supplies behind, returned to the creek. There Azcuenaga revived. The next day they awoke and started to walk. They spotted a farmhouse near McDermitt—the first sign of civilization in days. They continued walking until they reached the small town of Jordan Valley, Oregon, a few miles from the border of Idaho Territory.

Months later, Navarro and Azcuenaga, two of the first Basque immigrants to Idaho, returned to the spot in the desert where they had nearly died. They wanted the clothes they had left behind.[1]

On Saturday night, June 16, 1990, a bottleneck of humanity formed at the main entrance of the old Idaho State Penitentiary on the eastern side of Boise. It took ten minutes or more just to squeeze through the entrance, but inside, the view was remarkable. Lights shone down on thousands of people packed into what was called Lekeitio Plaza. Because of its resemblance to an Old Country village square, what once had been the main yard of the prison was chosen by the organizing committee as the site of Jaialdi '90, Idaho's International Basque Festival.

Near the entrance, on the festival's main stage, the band Ordago was playing rock with English and Basque lyrics, keeping the ocean of heads, arms, and legs moving. The crowd, braving the drizzle that was beginning to fall, bobbed up and down in waves or joined hands to skip in long, serpentine chains. The plaza was filled with a mixture of faces and features, from the old and worn, with etched lines like those of the traditional Basque wood carvings to blond, blue-eyed teenagers. In the bleachers that lined the dance area, older Basque women marked the music with their feet and watched to see who was dancing with whom. Others just rested on the periphery, leaning against the high sandstone walls, catching up with friends they had not seen in a long time or visiting with new acquaintances. At the far end of the dance area, revelers stood three-, four-, and five-deep at the bar waiting for drinks.

Smells of olive oil, garlic, and pimientos accented the air. Prodigious amounts of Basque and American food were prepared: *solomo* (pork loin), lamb, *churros* (deep-fried pastry), croquettes, beans, fish, pork chops with red peppers, and chorizo (the pork sausage popular among

Idahoans). There was every kind of souvenir: berets, *bota* bags, sweat-shirts, T-shirts, books, tapes, crafts, boats, hats, scarves, wind socks, stickers, posters, and flags—many of them bearing the Jaialdi logo of a dancer on one knee, twirling the Basque flag. Spectators who would not have been able to identify the Basque provinces on a map angled *txapelak* (Basque berets) on their heads and stumbled through impro-vised versions of the jota, a Basque fandango.

Many had been attracted by the advertisements in western maga-zines and newspapers that had trumpeted the Jaialdi '90 festival for weeks. They were hosted by nearly a thousand volunteers who attended to every detail, pouring beer, installing electrical lines, supplying first aid. Every one of these volunteers was needed: On the Saturday and Sunday of the festival, an estimated twenty-five thousand people emp-tied 210 kegs of Budweiser and ate an estimated five thousand pounds of chorizo.

At one point a visitor from the Basque Country looked down on the thousands jammed together, trying their best to dance in the limited space. She remarked, "I don't know where I am—Boise or the Basque Country."

The contrast of these two events depicts the evolution of the Basques in Idaho from poor, anonymous immigrants who literally staggered across the border. The Basque community grew to attract thousands to its eth-nic festival. This evolution occurred for many reasons, but perhaps a single Basque word summarizes it most effectively: *aukera*. In the first comprehensive Basque-English dictionary, *aukera* (pronounced ow-KEH-ruh) is defined as choice or selection and opportunity, chance, or possibility. Over the century that Basques have been in Idaho, the choices and opportunities of three generations have created a subcul-ture that is neither purely Basque nor purely American; it is Basque-American—unique, yet representing a tiny cross section of the common American experience.

Each generation is marked by the choices it made, and the opportu-nities offered, especially the immigrant generation, which made the most dramatic choice of all—to come to America. Basque men found oppor-tunities in sheepherding, a job no one else wanted. Although isolating and often miserable work, sheepherding matched the needs and abili-ties of Basque immigrants, most especially since they did not have to

know English. As one herder commented, "What the hell else was I going to do, work in an office?"[2] Even though few Basque immigrants
herded sheep back home, their agrarian background and values of hard
work, perseverance, and endurance allowed them to be successful in the
sheep business. As a result of the herding lifestyle, boardinghouses
emerged, and that in turn created opportunities for Basque women.
Most Basques came to Idaho in the first decades of the century, and
though restrictive immigration laws and an improved Basque economy
slowed the flow, a trickle remained steady until the 1970s. Though there
might have been more Basques in California or Argentina, their concentration in sparsely populated Idaho was highly noticeable.

When Basques arrived in Idaho, they stayed together. Basque immigrants worked, formed business partnerships, and married almost exclusively among themselves. Most of them arrived young and single,
and their common experiences so far from home helped them to forge
strong friendships. Compared to other ethnic groups that immigrated
to Idaho, Basques faced limited discrimination. Few distinguishing
racial characteristics separated them from their American neighbors.
Moreover, an agrarian culture that measured self-worth through hard
physical labor matched well with the American work ethic, and over
time the Basque immigrants earned the respect of Idahoans. Almost all
arrived with the idea of returning to the Basque Country after having
saved some money. Some did. Many, however, chose to stay. For some,
this decision may have come immediately, but for most it evolved slowly
as they grew accustomed to life in the United States. Those who stayed
created choices and opportunities for the next generation.

The second generation grew up as Basques at home and Americans
in public. Their immigrant parents worked hard to give them even
more possibilities and to instill in them good work habits and values
that, when coupled with an education, provided a solid base for a successful life in the United States. Many climbed the social ladder to become managers, bankers, lawyers, and entrepreneurs. In the process,
they became more American. They were part of a hyphenated American generation that came of age during World War II, that great Americanizing period.

Most second-generation Basques were not infused with tales of life
in the Basque Country and the difficult conditions that had motivated
their parents to leave homes and families forever. Instead, their focus was

on a promising look ahead. The Basque language, spoken almost universally by the first generation, was largely lost to the second, as children learned English in American schools. Some Americanized their names, moved away from Idaho, and married non-Basques. Others married Basques and never left their ethnic environment. The majority settled somewhere in between. Some of the second generation did preserve Basque traditions through dances, picnics, and sporting events. These choices kept certain cultural traits alive and set the stage for the third generation.

The third generation, the ethnic generation, developed during a period of immense change in the United States. During the 1960s and afterward, it became less fashionable to be simply American—living in what many considered to be a bland, vanilla culture—and increasingly popular to be *from* somewhere, to have an identity that set one apart. A preservation movement by a number of third-generation Basques in Idaho proved a theory proposed by sociologist Marcus Lee Hansen: "What the son [of immigrants] wishes to forget, the grandson wishes to remember." Whenever any immigrant group reaches the third generation, he wrote, "a spontaneous and almost irresistible impulse arises" that brings together different people from various backgrounds based on one common factor: "heritage—the heritage of blood."[3]

Unlike the first and second generations, whose blood boiled upon hearing epithets such as "black Basco!" the third generation proclaimed its pride on bumper stickers, license plates, and T-shirts: I'M A CUTE LITTLE BASQUE! PROUD TO BE BASQUE! BASQUING IN THE SUN! While some immigrants and children of immigrants Americanized their names from Enrique to Henry and José Mari to Joe, some of the third generation named their children Maite and Aitor. "To what degree do I take on the ways of America?"—the choice presented to the first generation—was inverted and became "To what degree do I take on the ways of Basque culture?" Their choices covered a wide spectrum; some kept virtually no ties to Idaho's Basque community, others moved to live in the Basque Country. In many ways, third-generation Basques had the best of both worlds; they could claim to be unique in the larger American society, yet still feel the security of a community, something that many Americans were lacking.

Though no one family story fits this three-generation theory perfectly, many resemble the story of the Bilbao family, used as an illustra-

tion throughout this book. But it is just one example of the stories of
the Basque experience in Idaho. All Basques, from the earliest days,
contributed to the formation of the subculture through their choices,
which were based upon opportunities available at the time. To understand the roots of this subculture, one must look back much further
than Navarro and Azcuenaga's trip across the desert—back through the
millennia of Basque history.

I

The Immigrant Generation

F rancisco "Frank" Ciriaco Bilbao was born in 1911 in Arrieta, Bizkaia, the only boy in the family until his mother adopted another son, Emilio. "She had me, my five sisters," he said. "But someone left a baby at church in a basket, and the nuns found him. My mother had lost a baby during childbirth, so she took this boy instead—Emilio. She adopted him." When Frank was eight, his father died in a rockslide while working on a road construction crew. "After that I didn't see too many good things for the future." Frank, who had attended school for only two years, learning the basics of reading and writing, then dropped out to help his mother, who was struggling to support the family as a seamstress.

At age eleven, Frank moved to San Palaio, about fifteen kilometers from his hometown, to work for some family friends. One of his most important jobs was to take care of San Juan de Gastelugatxe, a hermitage set atop a protruding cliff overlooking the Bay of Biscay. Almost every day for three years, he climbed the 365 steps leading to the top of the cliff so he could clean the chapel. Some days he would also lead a burro up the steps, cut the grass on the dizzying slopes that bordered the steps, load it on the burro, and take it home to feed the farm animals. "They paid me about sixteen dollars a year," Frank remembered. "All I got in my mind is, 'I got to help my mother.' All that money went there because I knew she needed it."

"When I was fourteen," Frank said, "this friend, he got me a job working on a boat. I made nine dollars a month transporting cargo all around the world. I've been to all the ports in Spain. I liked it—there was quite a difference from making sixteen dollars a year. That way, my mother got more help. That was her salvation. That was a pretty good job for someone like me—young, not too much education. But I knew my mother and me needed more."

Frank's adopted brother, Emilio, had emigrated to New York two years earlier and had found work in a restaurant. "I wanted to get on the boat coming to the United States," said Frank. He was seventeen when he finally got on a freighter headed to New York, making two ocean crossings before he and some friends decided to jump ship. "I was telling my mother I was gonna jump when I get the chance. She knew I was gonna send money to her, so she was praying I have good luck. We left in the dark, nighttime. They let you go to town for a few hours. I took two or three sets of clothes on my body and left most on the boat. I put all the clothes on I can." He was well padded by the extra layers of clothes. "By the time I got out of there, I was a pretty big boy! I was seventeen years old, just a kid. That was 1928."

After he had jumped ship in the New York harbor, Frank was met by his brother. "They caught a few of the guys who snuck off, but I was well hidden in town," he said. "Emilio found a job for me right where he was working. He was a cook, and he got me a job washing dishes. That was the jackpot for me. I was the luckiest guy in the whole country. How lucky a person can be: jump ship and have those kind of conveniences. I was tickled to death to have a job, a place to stay. I think a lot of times, if kids went through what I went through, that would have been better than a high school education for them."

⊨ ⊨

F rank worked for six months washing dishes. "I saved every bit of it. I sent a cashier's check to my mother in a registered letter. New York was a good moneymaking area then." He stayed at a Basque boardinghouse. "I had nice room to sleep in. I met other guys like me—ship jumpers." Though he had been successful in New York, he was still nervous that he would be arrested for being an illegal immigrant. "I was a-shakin'," he said, "afraid of getting caught every hour of every day. Every time I see a uniform I was scared to death they were gonna pick me up."

He had heard from other Basques that there were sheepherding jobs available in the West, and he even had some friends from back home who were living in Idaho. He decided it would be safer and more lucrative if he moved there. But he still had to make the train trip. He saved his dishwashing money for the fare of ninety-eight dollars. "Paid everything cash." Before he left, he was still nervous about being recognized as an illegal alien, but Valentin Aguirre, the owner of the Casa Vizcaína boardinghouse in New York, gave him advice. "He told me, 'You're young, and people will think you're not from here. You gotta get an English newspaper in front of you all the time, and you gotta look like you're reading. Don't make anyone suspicious. When they stop the train, and everyone's getting in and getting out, you always gotta be watchin' those policemen. You get that paper in front of you, and you act like you're readin' it.' And that's what I did."

Worries of arrest made the trip across the country to Idaho seem an eternity. "I never did know the time of arrival [in Boise] or anything like that. We ate a sandwich every once in a while. The trip took about three days, maybe four. When we got to Boise, well, I was tickled to death when I saw two friends of mine at the station. When I saw them there, I thought, 'This is my home.'" Benito Ysursa, the owner of the Modern Hotel on Idaho Street, also met Frank and his Basque traveling companion at the train depot in Boise. "We told Ben [Benito], 'We ain't got no money, and we want to go to work.'"

After sending his mother his savings from New York and paying for train fare to Idaho, Frank had only forty dollars left. "Ben said, 'Don't worry about it,' and he pat me on the back. 'If you need money, I support you and you can pay me back later.' And I couldn't believe that," Frank remembered. Benito took them to the Modern Hotel, where they were given room and board in exchange for cleaning up around the boardinghouse. "We stayed there two or three days. We never did have any money, but we got a lot of credit."

"I wanted to stay in Boise," Frank recalled. "But we heard Andy Little was hiring men in Emmett." Andy Little was a Scot who had immigrated to Idaho and become one of the most important sheepmen in the West. He had grown to prefer Basque sheepherders because of their dependability and their success with sheep. It was mid-March, the tail end of the lambing season, and there was a high demand for labor. Frank went to the bus depot. "I find out that one of the bus drivers was a Basco. I tell him, 'Bunch of us here, we want to go to Emmett, we goin' to work for Andy Little.' So this guy says, 'Anytime you ready, I take you down. We go to Emmett.'"

Soon after arriving in Emmett, Frank found work with Andy Little's sheep company. He was hired for forty dollars a month to herd sheep, something he had never done before. "But I had an advantage from the city slickers," he said. "Being in the mountains [in the Basque Country] made a lot of difference. I was a mountaineer over there too. But over there people only have maybe seventy-five to eighty head of sheep." He now had to watch over more than two thousand head all by himself.

In late March 1929, Frank started driving his sheep to the mountains of the Boise and Payette National Forests and quickly discovered that it would not be an easy task. "I have a lot of dark days, more than I can explain. I cry many times too. I had a few moments that if I had a chance, I take a train and a boat and I go home. I was thinkin' of home, my family, my sisters. It was lonely. You only got a visit 'bout once a week."

Occasionally, he made contact with Ignacio Pagoaga, an older, more experienced herder. "I was his kind of person. That man, Ignacio, he always treat me like his own son. That's why [herding] was easier for me, having him to tell me how to work the sheep: 'Frank, if you want to save a lot of work, get up early in morning. Get those sheep before they start movin' from their bed ground and always have a place ready for the next day.' And that's exactly what I did. But a lot of people sleep late and then the sheep start going over here, some over there—then the herder doesn't know which way to go. Those are the guys that have a problem. Don't do any good for Andy Little, don't do any good for nobody."

Another problem he had to overcome was the predators—even bears. "Those bears, they would get one or two lambs today, a few tomorrow. I was thinkin', 'Jesus Christ, if this stays that way, I'll be out of a job. I've got to do something to get rid of them. They're scarin' the sheep.' I was scared to death." So Frank rigged a trap. He attached a piece of meat to a cord, then attached the other end to the trigger of his shotgun, which he pointed so bears would shoot themselves. "The bear would grab that meat and pull that trigger—BOOM!—hit him right in there in the chest. I killed a lot of bears that way. I saved Andy Little a few head of sheep doing that. Those bears do a lot of damage."

Frank confronted other problems his first year herding sheep. One day he was herding in Scott Valley near Cascade. "My camptender went to town and left me alone. A few of my sheep started to wander over to this farmer's land. I didn't know any different, but Andy Little didn't rent that pasture from this farmer's land. Pretty soon, I saw these dogs running up to the sheep, and then I saw a man with a rifle in his hand, a couple of kids maybe fourteen or fifteen years old with him. He's coming to me, and he says something to me. I had a rifle in my hands, but I put it down. I looked at them, but I couldn't understand what they were talking about. This guy grabbed me and put the rifle in my chest. Then this man started hitting me with his rifle, and there was blood coming from my face, and I just started running and I ran to my camp about one mile from there. I got in my tent and I sat there, crying."

Frank rarely went into Emmett, because there were too many money-spending temptations for a sheepherder who was determined to save. "I would go to town maybe once or twice a year. I would write a few lines on a letter and send the money to my mother, because I knew she needed it and I was plannin' on goin' back to Arrieta. I sent everything. One month, I had no money, old clothes, old pants, and I asked Andy Little for a fifty-dollar [advance] check. I looked at his big mustache, and he was thinking. It was 1930. At that time, most of the banks in America were closed. Andy Little got his purse out—he had a bunch of twenty-dollar bills in there—got the money out, gave it to the camptender, he gave it to me. He told me checks were no good. All the banks were closed. That was Saturday. About four or five of us sheepherders decided to go to town. I buy everything! Shoes, socks, everything I needed—and a gallon of whiskey for four of us."

On these rare occasions when he went to Emmett, Frank stayed at the Charchas Boardinghouse. "I enjoyed my times in Emmett," he said. "We never had no money. But these girls, young girls, that worked at this boardinghouse were nice. They got a [jukebox], you know. It took a nickel. We'd put a nickel in it, and we would start dancing with the girls." Frank said that everybody wanted to continue dancing even after they ran out of nickels. "The girls wanted to dance too. So they took the nickels out of the jukebox and put 'em back in. We really enjoyed that."

Frank met his wife, Frances, at one of these Emmett boardinghouse dances. "I had seen lots of good-lookin' girls, maybe better than [Frances], but I must have been in love," he joked with Frances years later. She answered, "Do you know why he liked me? I wore bib overalls and . . . he knew I would be a hard worker, that's why he liked me. I was just a fifteen-year-old kid, a teenager, when he was over there with those girls at the other boardinghouses, the ones who took the nickels out of the jukebox. We knew each other for about a year and then got married in 1936. Frank didn't speak any English and I didn't speak any Spanish, so we spoke Basque all the time. His name was Francisco, but I always called him Frank, from day one."

"Right after the honeymoon," Frances remembered, "we went straight to the lambing shed. That was in January, around the middle of January." While her new husband worked in the shed, she took a job as a cook, supplying meals for the exhausted men.

+═ ═+

Frances Bilbao told of her own family's immigration into the United States. Her mother, Maria Dolores, moved to Idaho from the Bizkaian village of Ondarroa in January 1915. She was twenty-three years old. On the train ride west, Maria Dolores saw the first black man she had ever seen. He was chewing tobacco. ("That's how it works," Frances said her mother concluded. "Black people spit black.") When her mother arrived in Idaho, Frances Bilbao said, her sister, Maria Cruz, already had picked a boyfriend for her—Eugenio Bicandi (nicknamed Torero because he worked with bulls on a ranch). Eugenio was from Ibarruri, Bizkaia, just a few miles from Maria Dolores's hometown, Ondarroa. Ironically, they met in Idaho, seven thousand miles away; within months, they were married. They later opened a boardinghouse in Emmett, where their daughter Frances eventually met her future husband.

"My mother and father bought this boardinghouse in Emmett in 1925," Frances Bilbao said. "I was eight years old when we moved in. I was the oldest of five and we had moved from Barber to Emmett when the sawmill moved. I didn't know any English when I first went to school, because every other house around where we lived in Barber was Basque. I had to do the first grade twice. Another Basque girl from the neighborhood and I were always getting into trouble at school, because we didn't know what was going on. The teacher would tell us to sit down, and when we wouldn't settle down, we would get hit with this long willow stick.

"The boardinghouse work was tough. My mother had no washing machine and five kids and still had to clean all the linens. It was tough for my dad too. I remember my dad selling whiskey during Prohibition. Local professionals would buy it. Then somebody turned Dad in. The police came in at night, we kids had the door to the boardinghouse locked. My mother poured some of the stuff down the toilet, and I think she even tried to hide some of it in the beds."

⇥ ⇤

F rank Bilbao had always planned to return to the Basque Country to live. He had been in the United States for eight years, the whole time sending money back home, hoping to use it as the base for a successful return. Now, in the mid-1930s, he had an American-born Basque wife, and it looked as if he was going to remain in the United States. And there was another reason to stay. By 1936, civil war was erupting in Spain, a war that would change the future of the Basque Country. "When the war broke out, I thought, 'What am I gonna do over there? I would have to go to the service.'" Compared with the suffering that Basques would face in their homeland, working in a lambing shed seemed like a good alternative.

In the late 1930s, Frank decided he had had enough of sheepherding. He found a job at a sawmill in Emmett, and he and Frances lived at her parents' boardinghouse for two years, helping with the everyday boardinghouse chores. "I butchered a seven-hundred-pound pig with Frances's father once," Frank recalled. "We bought it for $6.50. We made close to two thousand chorizos with that pig."

Though the boardinghouse life was difficult, it also seemed like a good opportunity for a business, Frank thought. He heard that a dam was going to be constructed near the small logging town of Cascade, about seventy-five miles north of Boise. Many workers, including Basques, would be moving to Cascade, and they would need a place to stay. "What else could I do?" Frank asked. "With a family, you don't go into the sheep business unless you are an owner. There was a big boom coming to Cascade. I made up my mind this would be the best for us." So Frank decided to get into the boardinghouse business. "We came up [to Cascade] in the dead of winter," Frances Bilbao said, "about two years before they started building the new dam, and we bought the old Emery Hotel. It was the dumpiest thing that you'd ever want to be in. It had fifteen bedrooms, one toilet upstairs, no bath, just a shower, and one toilet downstairs, and that was the size of the thing—and we bought it. We paid twelve thousand dollars for it. It was hard to buy lumber and other supplies during the war years. I was buying stuff black market. But we did it. We also built the bar, and it was nothing but hard work from then on.

"I had always said to myself, when I was a girl growing up in a boardinghouse, that I would never, never end up in a boardinghouse again," she said. "And look where I ended up."

After Frank and Frances had adequately restored the Emery Hotel to open for business and built the Valley Club bar, off to one side of the hotel, they were prepared for the boom in Cascade. "When the dam came in there was a lot of construction for a while," Frances said. "The hours were long. *Bearrik ez dago besterik* [Work, there's no other way]. I was packing twelve or fourteen lunches for the Basque guys who were going to work every day. I was cooking their meals, plus the food for the fellows we hired in the bar, because it was open twenty-four hours a day for the first years, until Idaho stopped that. We had slot machines, we had a roulette table, we had blackjack, we had a poker table. Bascos did most of the operating."

Frank and Frances worked the exhausting hours seven days a week, but they made the Emery Hotel a successful venture. "*Zer da vacacinue?* [What's a vacation?] We never took a vacation. Work—that's what we did. We didn't play very much, we didn't have time to play. When you don't play, you save money, and when you save it, you can invest it." The decision to move to Cascade had been a good one. Frank said, "All my decisions, somebody been helping me—God, or somebody."

1

An Ancient People

Basques in Idaho trace their heritage to north-central Spain and southwestern France, a tiny corner of Europe that has been occupied by humans for the last seventy thousand years. For centuries historians, anthropologists, linguists, philologists, and folklorists have tried to determine whether those early inhabitants were the original Basques, but attempts to find the origins and identity of the Basques have often resembled the efforts of medieval cartographers drawing a map of the world, with small islands of proof becoming large landmasses of speculation and guesswork often substituting for fact. Many simply label the Basques "the mystery people of Europe" and suggest that we may never know their origin. Still, even the most conservative interpretation shows that Basques lived in this rather wet, mountainous area by 5000 to 3000 B.C., making them the oldest permanent residents of Western Europe.[1]

This area today is known as Euskal Herria and comprises seven regions (formerly referred to as provinces in the literature on Basques) straddling the westernmost portion of the Franco-Spanish border along the Pyrenees mountain range. It fills 20,600 square kilometers, no more than New Jersey, stretching fewer than a hundred miles at its farthest points.[2] Because of the area's long history of foreign intrusion and internal division, however, it would be inaccurate to describe these regions as a unified country. The three northernmost regions—Lapurdi, Behenafarroa, and Zuberoa—have been part of France since the early sixteenth century. The four southern regions—Araba, Bizkaia, Gipuzkoa, and Navarre—are part of Spain and have had their own internal divisions for centuries. The largest and southernmost of these, Navarre, was for hundreds of years the heart of a powerful kingdom that experienced a unique history. In Araba longtime relations with Castile, the geographical and political center of Spain, contributed to a steady erosion of Basque culture and language. Even in coastal, mountainous Bizkaia and Gipuzkoa, which are bastions of Basque tradition, industrialization brought migrants from all corners of Spain, who settled and attempted to obscure the notion of a clear Basque identity.[3]

Although the Basques' area of cultural hegemony has contracted, nationalists have argued that there is a separate Basque race that has had rights to these seven regions for thousands of years. In the 1930s, at the entrance of a cave in Gipuzkoa, two Basque anthropologists found a skull that dated to 1500 B.C. and displayed typical Basque traits, particularly broad at the top and narrow at the bottom. Basques have also shown an unusually high proportion (up to 42 percent in one survey) of Rh-negative blood, which indicates a lengthy, continuous occupation in the area. Their strongest identifier, Euskera, the Basque language, has unknown roots and cannot be linked with any Indo-European languages, though linguists have long attempted to compare it with tongues as diverse as Hungarian and Japanese.

The unique language, the blood and bone evidence, and the absence of a migration legend in Basque folklore prompt many scholars to conclude that Basques are the sole survivors of Europe's aboriginal population and that they were living in this region long before 2000 B.C., when Indo-Europeans began to enter the continent, bringing with them the traditions and languages that shaped Europe.[4]

The data allow historians to argue with greater certainty that Basques occupied the area long before the Roman legions entered the Iberian Peninsula around 200 B.C. During the seven centuries of Roman domination in the peninsula, relations with the Basques were for the most part peaceful. The Basques apparently accepted Roman hegemony in return for local autonomy. In many respects, their best defense against complete Roman occupation, as it would be against other foreign threats, was the remoteness of their rocky, steep land. Judging by the records of Roman authors, it appears that the Basques during this period lived isolated in narrow green river valleys, divided into four main tribes that spoke dialects of a common Basque language.[5]

Yet Basques were not entirely free of Roman influence. The Romans left behind clear architectural remains, most notably roads and bridges, and they gave the region its first exposure to Christianity, though Basques would be the last people in southwestern Europe to convert. Euskera acquired Roman agricultural and commercial terms, and words of Latin origin are still scattered throughout the Basque language. Some historians even suggest that the Basque language might have disappeared altogether if the Romans had controlled the area for several more centuries.[6]

Roman influence declined, however, and "barbarian" tribes supplanted the Romans throughout Europe. By the sixth century, Basque territory was divided into two regions of foreign control: the Franks dominated an area corresponding to the modern French Basque region and northern Navarre, and the Visigoths, facing a great deal of opposition, seized Araba, Bizkaia, and Gipuzkoa. It was a division that stuck. While Navarre defeated the Franks and became an independent kingdom in the tenth century, Araba, Bizkaia, and Gipuzkoa clashed with the Goths and their successors, the kings of Castile and Leon. Travelers by this time clearly recognized the uniqueness of the Basques. One described them as "different from others both in their customs and in their race." Other descriptions were less flattering: "swarthy, ugly-faced . . . perverse . . . drunken." Their unique language, another writer claimed, sounded "like dogs barking."[7]

As the kings were attempting to unify the Iberian Peninsula's mosaic of regions and kingdoms, Basques developed a relatively civilized society, and by the end of the Middle Ages the liberties enjoyed by common Basques would be the envy of other Europeans. Serfdom disappeared in the Basque Country before any other region in Spain. Even though they were slow to convert, Basques eventually embraced Catholicism, a tradition that peaked in the sixteenth and seventeenth centuries with the achievements of Saint Ignatius of Loyola, founder of the Jesuit order, and Saint Francis Xavier, the renowned missionary to Asia.

Though the Basque region was the last in Europe to organize into municipalities, early political bodies known as *batzarrak* became an effective form of governing Basque communities.[8] Basques developed an advanced democratic system that was recognized to varying degrees by Spanish kings until 1876, shortly before Basques first began emigrating to Idaho. This self-governance was guaranteed by the *foruak,* one of the most important elements for Basque independence. The *foruak* were specific agreements with the king of Spain, usually made on a regional level, an exchange of loyalty to the crown for local autonomy. Codified by the fourteenth century, the *foruak* offered Basques a high degree of freedom, predating by several centuries the liberties that British colonists would demand during the American Revolution. The regional governing council levied taxes, controlled soldiers, and even reviewed laws submitted by the king; Gipuzkoans and Bizkaians could veto any of these laws by proclaiming: "We obey but do not comply." In addition, the Bizkaian agreement required the Spanish monarch to travel to the town of Gernika and swear obedience to the *foruak* beneath a large oak tree, which became known as the Tree of Gernika. The Basques kept their *foruak* longer than any other region in Spain, earning them a reputation as lovers of democracy and independence. John Adams, the second president of the United States, wrote that though their neighbors had suffered an erosion of autonomy, the Basques had "preserved their ancient language, genius, laws, government, and manners without innovation longer than any other nation in Europe."[9]

Over the centuries, however, a more subtle invader crossed into the Basque Country, slowly stealing away the cultural and political independence that Basques enjoyed. In many ways, their own commercial success, culminating during the Industrial Revolution, was the most dangerous threat to Basque identity. Basques became the victims of their own industrial progress, for they were increasingly viewed by the governing monarchy as indispensable contributors to the Spanish nation-state. As Spain unified and extended its power around the world, Basques in the fifteenth to sixteenth centuries were instrumental in its success at all stages, supplying resources and their vast maritime knowledge. Basque navigators and crews played key roles in many of the major voyages of discovery, including those of Christopher Columbus, Amerigo Vespucci, and Vasco Nuñez de Balboa. One Basque, Juan Sebastián Elcano, took charge of the first circumnavigation of the globe in 1521 after Magellan was killed in the Philippines. The Basque region, especially Bizkaia, became renowned for its iron production, and Queen Isabella I contracted Basque shipbuilders to construct boats that would sail all over the globe; between 1520 and 1580 almost 80 percent of ship traffic to the New World was controlled by Basques.[10]

By the late-nineteenth century, an upper class of Basque industrialists had an interest in maintaining a strong Spanish state. Basque society, which had survived foreign invasion and war, split between these new industrialists in the cities and the conservative farmers in rural areas. This split mirrored a larger division within the entire Spanish state that exploded into war over the question of succession to the throne after Fernando VII died in 1833. The Carlist wars of the nineteenth century exacerbated the division between the rural traditionalists and the liberal industrialists and meant the end of the *foruak*.[11]

Despite the two Carlist wars, the Basques, enjoying an industrial boom, formed closer economic ties with Spain. Bizkaia and Gipuzkoa, with their ample supplies of iron, urbanized and industrialized faster and to a greater extent than most anywhere else in Spain. From 1875 to 1895 Bizkaian iron production increased twenty times to accommodate the demands of the thousands of miles of railway being built throughout the world. By the end of the nineteenth century, Spain produced 21.5 percent of the world's iron ore, most of it coming from Bizkaia. Workers from all regions of Spain migrated to Basque cities; Bizkaia's population exploded from 112,000 in 1840 to 190,000 in 1868. The Basque upper class began to align itself with the Madrid government, and bankers, factory owners, and insurance companies saw little advantage in upholding Basque tradition and autonomy. On the contrary, there was much to be gained financially by joining the larger Spanish political and economic unit.[12] The new wealth of the Basque elite created a natural resentment among the lower and middle classes, who had to contend with overcrowding, pollution, and other problems of industrialization without enjoying its benefits. Industrialization and Spanish immigration also had a disastrous effect on Basque language and culture; by the beginning of the twentieth century the Basque language had mostly disappeared in Araba and Navarre, except in the northern villages of Navarre. The developing resentment of the rural population and a segment of the urban middle classes, and the fear that the ancient traditions would become extinct, created a desire among lower-class Basques to proclaim their uniqueness. This resulted in the first faltering steps of the movement for an independent Basque nation, encouraged by an unlikely leader, Sabino Arana.[13]

Arana, born near Bilbao in 1865, spoke only Spanish as a child, spent most of his formative years hundreds of miles from the Basque Country, and died at age thirty-eight. Nevertheless, he became the founder of

Basque nationalism and the main proponent of the revival of Euskera. While living in Barcelona as a young student, Arana, influenced by the Catalan independence movement, grew impassioned enough about the Basque cause to devote his short life to it. His was a Herculean task. By the 1890s Spanish immigration had overtaken Basque urban areas, and Euskera seemed destined for extinction. Although he did not study the Basque language until late in his teens, Arana began his movement by promoting its use. He wrote newspaper and magazine articles in Euskera and published Basque grammar and history texts. Adamant about purging Euskera of Spanish influence, he went so far as to create his own Basque words, some of which did not catch on—*txadon* for church, for example—and some of which are still used today, such as *aberri* for country.[14]

Equally important to Arana was the purification of the Basque race. He detested Spaniards, calling them "the people of blasphemy," and condemned Basques who married them, saying they had "confounded themselves with the most vile and despicable race in Europe." When he established his Basque centers, *batzokiak,* to spread nationalism, he divided members into three categories according to their Basque ancestry. Only those with four Basque grandparents could hold executive office.[15]

To Arana, the most important idea was the preservation of Basque traditions and values, and the only way to ensure this was to form a nation. He even created a new name for this state, Euzkadi (later Euskadi), a reunion of the seven Basque regions including the three "lost" to France. Arana designed the Basque flag, which was red, white, and green in the pattern of the Union Jack. By the time he died in 1903, he had achieved little politically, but he left an important legacy, including the Basque Nationalist Party, which would dominate Basque politics throughout the twentieth century. More important, he had created a new ideology, which asserted that Basques were a separate race with unique customs and should, therefore, be allowed to govern their own state.[16]

Arana's movement was largely urban and middle class. The people whose lives he wanted all Basques to emulate, those who followed traditional Basque folkways in the rural areas, were largely isolated from the fledgling tenets of his nationalism. They were plowing with oxen, cutting grass on slopes with scythes, devoting themselves to the Catholic Church as they had for centuries. Rural people were slow to embrace the new ideas of separation and nationalism; they were more concerned with earning a living than with debating what it meant to be Basque. These farmers and fishermen were the ones who would emigrate to Idaho. They missed much of the explosive history that would shape the modern Basque Country and instead brought with them to Idaho their agrarian way of life, work ethic, democratic values, and religious faith, which had been evolving over thousands of years.[17]

The Makeup of the Immigrant

Older Basques in Idaho often kept photographs taken when their grandparents or great-grandparents were young. The photographs might be sober turn-of-the-century wedding portraits, the groom seated, the bride standing at his side, sometimes wearing black in keeping with the custom to mourn a full year after the death of a relative. Or it might be a late-nineteenth-century family picture, featuring as many as four generations in front of a stone farmhouse, everyone dressed in their best town clothes, the future for the young clearly etched in the faces of the old.

At the end of the twentieth century, not far from any town in Bizkaia, passing over hills covered with damp ferns and pine trees, one can see traces of life as it was for the people in these photographs, and for generations before them: roads not wide enough for two cars and farmhouses with rough walls built long before the signing of the Declaration of Independence. Heavy doors open to the aromas of garlic, peppers, and onions from the kitchen and damp hay from the stable. In the distance, jagged mountains poke through wet clouds, and below are small towns dominated by the steeples of churches, settled into narrow green valleys or tucked into the folds of the coast.[18]

The first Basque immigrants to Idaho came from rural surroundings like these, from inland Markina and Gernika or from Lekeitio and Ondarroa on the coast, from villages with no more than a few dozen or a few hundred people. They grew up in *baserriak,* chaletlike farmhouses first built in the 1700s and still common today. These *baserriak* and the land that surrounds them reflect the core of rural Basque identity. Each *baserri* conforms to its geographical surroundings and generally consists of two or three stories, with flat roofs and exposed beams. Often these farmhouses contain living quarters and a stable or other working areas built as one unit. Because there is so little arable land in the region, the property around each *baserri* is small, usually six to ten hectares, and frequently positioned on the side of a hill.[19]

Until the mid-twentieth century, these *baserriak* offered subsistence living for farmers struggling to grow a variety of crops in the wet maritime climate. Through the centuries Basques in rural areas developed a practical yet ingenious system of self-sufficiency. They drank cider made from apples grown in their own orchards, ate eggs and cheese produced by their own animals, sweetened their food with honey from their own beehives, and wore socks and jackets made of wool sheared from their own sheep. Cash, always in short supply and usually earned from the sale of animals or the surplus of their small gardens, was spent frugally, used almost exclusively for dowries or for rent. *Baserritarrak* were easy to identify, the men with their *abarketak* (rope-soled shoes with a canvas top that laced up almost to the knees) and the women clad in long, dark dresses and scarves tied with two tight knots that protruded from the top of their heads.[20]

There was a deep contrast between these *baserritarrak* and the fishermen, according to Joe Eiguren, who spent most of his early years in the coastal town of Lekeitio. "There was a difference in language and attitudes, and their likes and dislikes about each other." Dialectical variations and occupational pride exaggerated these distinctions, which carried over even to their clothing. The fishermen wore baggy cotton trousers and wool sweaters for the rapidly changing weather. While fishing, they donned wooden clogs, and as they walked to the port before dawn, their tramping echoed through town. All men, both fishermen and farmers, wore a black or dark-blue *txapela,* or beret, one for workdays and another, usually edged with a band, for Sundays. Except at mass or meals, men wore the *txapelak* at all times. Joe Eiguren claimed, "If you washed your hands, you would take [the *txapela*] off and dry them with it."[21]

For both farmers and fishermen, life was dominated by hard labor and the Roman Catholic Church. Schooling was a luxury enjoyed by few, and a good education did not necessarily earn a person the respect of the community. Rural Basques honored a life of hard work and granted the highest respect to those who were successful through their own physical strength and stamina. The hard work of the *baserri,* anthropologist William A. Douglass wrote, was considered "wholesome" and "prestigious," and the *baserritarrak* believed in upholding their agricultural traditions not only for economic reasons but also for moral ones. Those Basques who went to Idaho exported with them this regard for work, providing the basis for much of the success they would enjoy in their new country.[22]

If they took a day off, it was usually a Sunday or a Catholic holy day. Many towns held Sunday dances, at which municipal bands would play in kiosks. At the turn of the century, Joe Eiguren said, the band from Lekeitio "played the same six songs every week." They would strike up two songs, take a break to give people a chance to stroll and visit, then two more songs, another break, and the final two songs. With priests serving as quiet but stifling chaperones, there were no waltzes or other dances that created physical contact between men and women; the band played group dances or jotas. Groups of men, especially the older ones, wandered to the bars and cafés to drink wine and play cards. Most women never entered bars and drank only on the grandest occasions.[23]

Except for these rare celebrations, life for rural Bizkaian Basques around the turn of the century was an unending series of grueling tasks endured simply to stay above the poverty level. Moreover, as Bizkaia industrialized, life became even harder. The advanced standard of living in urban areas created a setting where a subsistence life was not good enough and degraded the honorable position the Basque farmer once held. The *baserritarrak* found themselves in competition with larger agricultural enterprises, and, situated as they were on small plots of steep land, their capacity for expansion and modernization was limited.[24]

The materialism and competition of industrialization added to a problem that had long confronted young Basques growing up on these farms. For centuries, partly to avoid fragmenting the limited land, rural Basque families had followed a system in which the father selected one son or daughter (in Bizkaia, it was usually the firstborn) as the sole inheritor of the farm. The other siblings were usually free to stay on the farm, but they would have to obey the heir or heiress and remain celibate for life. Since Basques traditionally had large families, many children who were not fortunate enough to be the heir to the *baserri* were left with few choices for their future.[25]

One possibility for them was to join the tide of people flowing into Bilbao or a neighboring industrial town to work in factories or on the docks, but most rural Basques detested city life. The *kaletarrak,* urban dwellers, were rootless and lived in squalor. Basque peasants moving to the city would likely be surrounded by undesirable *maketoak* (poor Spanish immigrants) or by elite Basques who regarded them as backward and brutish. By the late 1890s, most jobs in Bilbao were low-paying, partly because Spain's economy suffered as it lost its vast imperial territories—Cuba, Puerto Rico, the Philippines. Because economic relations with the former colonies were terminated or curtailed, the Spanish economy slid into recession and, by 1908, into depression.[26]

Another choice for rural Basques was to leave the country and work temporarily elsewhere. Emigration had been an alternative for young Basques since Spain began building its empire; for centuries thousands had left to make their fortunes overseas, especially in South America. While Basque industries were forced to draw workers from distant corners of Spain, young Basque men from nearby farms emigrated to work across the ocean. As Sabino Arana and other early Basque nationalists labored to block the infusion of Spanish culture into Euskadi, thousands of young *baserritarrak* (in Arana's eyes, the "purest" Basques) left to find success overseas. "They were," Joe Eiguren said, "indifferent about nationalism and Sabino Arana and all that. They were just Basque, and they were proud to be Basque, but they didn't know why they were proud." Most were not concerned with the survival of Basque culture; they were preoccupied with their own survival.[27]

From Whaling to Herding

Although Basques have a reputation for loving their country, they also have a tradition of leaving it. Since at least the 1920s, Idahoans, both Basque and non-Basque, have claimed that their state is home to "the largest group of Basques anywhere on earth, except in their own native country in the Pyrenees."[28] The long history of Basque migration to all corners of the New World refutes that claim, however. It has always been difficult to obtain an accurate count of Basque migration into any country; either they were considered French or Spanish nationals or they "jumped ship," entering illegally, and were never counted at all. It is still clear, however, that their movement into the American West represents a relatively minor portion of Basque migration worldwide over several centuries.[29]

The Basques had established a history of exploration long before the great voyages of the Age of Discovery. In the seventh century they became Europe's first whalers, and as one Dutch scholar has suggested, by the 1500s their monopoly of the whale oil trade was comparable to the late-twentieth-century oil monopoly of the OPEC nations. Their search for whales took them to bodies of water as distant as the Greenland coasts, and there is some evidence that they fished for cod off the Grand Banks near Newfoundland long before Columbus arrived in America.[30]

After the discovery of the New World, Basque exploration was replaced by a tradition of colonial settlement. A seventeenth-century document complained that the population of Bizkaia was 75 percent female because so many men had left for the New World, never to return. Basques spread throughout the Spanish colonies to create the earliest communities in what would become Mexico, Uruguay, Colombia, and Venezuela. One Basque explorer founded the northern Mexican province of Nueva Vizcaya, naming its capital after his Bizkaian birthplace, Durango. Another Basque descendant became even more famous: Simón Bolívar, the liberator of South America.[31]

They succeeded almost everywhere they settled, in commerce, in agriculture, in mining. In the 1800s Basques became involved in the Latin American sheep industry, especially in its earliest development in the pampas of Argentina. Although they had had no experience herding large flocks of sheep back home, by the 1840s Basques were controlling the industry in Argentina's most important grazing areas.[32] The experience of these Basque sheepherders in Argentina indirectly established the basis for the flow of Basques into Idaho. The earliest Basques in the United States came not from Europe but from South America, where they had heard of the California Gold Rush in the mid-nineteenth century. Few Basques succeeded in gold mining in California, but many decided to stay and, drawing upon their herding experience in South America, benefited from a boom in the state's sheep industry. California Basques created a pattern that would be repeated several decades later in Idaho. A Basque would herd sheep and get settled enough to notify family and friends of employment opportunities, which led to the process of chain migration, one immigrant assisting the immigration of others.[33] Basques in California were generally from the French regions and Navarre in Spain, while Basques in Idaho and northern Nevada were almost exclusively from Bizkaia. Similar patterns could be found in smaller communities in Utah, Oregon, Wyoming, and other western states.

By the late-nineteenth century, almost every small town in the Basque Country had had at least one success story in the Americas, where possibilities for wealth seemed limitless if one was willing to invest several years of hard work, which was already a fact of life in the Old Country. Even if one was fortunate enough to inherit the family farm, there was no room for expansion. In the United States there were thousands of miles of grazing land barely trod upon. Sheepmen began to expand their grazing land beyond California into Nevada, where the range spread northward as a result of the completion of the transcontinental railroad. By the late 1880s Antonio Azcuenaga and José Navarro had struggled across the desert of northern Nevada to Jordan Valley, Oregon. During the summer of 1889 Azcuenaga guided his sheep up the Owyhee Mountains, crossing into what was still the Idaho Territory. "Thus," one author wrote, "it can be rightfully said that the Basques followed the sheep into Idaho."[34]

Some evidence suggests that Basques had been in Idaho before this. A Bizkaian woman, Narcissa Gestal, is said to have operated a florist shop at 224 East Idaho Street in Boise sometime before herders entered Idaho Territory. There is more proof that a man with a Basque surname, Jesus Urquides, came to the Boise Valley even earlier. Urquides, a packer, made his first trip to Boise in the early 1860s and, benefiting from the discovery of gold near Boise, developed a thriving business supplying the miners with equipment. He later packed ammunition for troops fighting in the 1878 Bannock Indian War. But Urquides was always identified as Spanish; his base camp off Main Street in Boise was called the Spanish Village.[35]

By the early 1890s, however, it is certain that Basques were moving north from Nevada, and a handful of Basques undertook the torturous desert crossing. In 1891 José Uberuaga, along with two companions, left on foot from Reno and walked through the desert to Boise. By the turn of the century more Basques began coming directly from Europe, traveling west across the United States by the transcontinental railroad. They represented the earliest pioneers on a journey that would be repeated by thousands over the following decades.[36]

From today's distant perspective, it appears that South America would have been a more attractive destination for a young Basque than the isolated and largely uncharted Idaho Territory. At the turn of the century Basques were well established in almost every country in South

America, where young men could likely find a well-connected relative or a family friend and could easily communicate in Spanish. Also, in 1898 the United States was at war with Spain, and a young Basque immigrant, once he had been labeled a Spaniard by Idahoans, would have faced the full brunt of a prejudice stoked by the national press (similar to what Germans and Japanese would encounter in later decades). It seems illogical that Basques would move to a country with an unfamiliar language, a country in which they might face harassment or violence.[37]

One explanation for the decision to immigrate to Idaho could be the rumors in Spain that the Latin American boom was over, that land in the pampas was too expensive for a poor emigrant. In light of such rumors, the newer sheepherding boom in Idaho looked more attractive. Basques viewed sheepherding in Idaho as a good opportunity to make money. The goal was not to be comfortable but to return to the Basque Country as wealthy and as quickly as possible. By the late 1890s there was already somewhat of a base for Basques in Idaho.[38]

2

The Trip to Idaho

The world had never experienced, and may never experience again, a migration quite like the one that took place during the decades straddling the turn of the twentieth century. From 1880 to 1920 more than twenty-three million immigrants, most of them southern and eastern Europeans, streamed into American ports of entry. By the end of that period almost a quarter of the total white population of the United States comprised people who had been born to foreign parents. They clustered in urban ghettos and windswept outposts, often following the paths of others from their hometowns. Among the many places they settled, Italians found their way to New York, Croatians to Pennsylvania, Germans to Wisconsin, and Basques to Idaho.[1]

During the first decade of the twentieth century, when total immigration into the United States reached its peak of 8.8 million, the small Basque community forming in Idaho also expanded, and by 1910, 999 Basques were recorded in the total state population of 300,000. Most of the early Basque immigrants to Idaho were males under thirty, more than 96 percent of them from Bizkaia. More than three-quarters were single, and of those who were married, half had left their wives behind. They did not have much money (fifty-three Boise-bound Basques who arrived in New York between 1897 and 1902 brought an average of $36.50) and were not well educated. In 1910 only 50.9 percent of the Basques in Idaho were able to read and write.[2]

Their trips were long and riddled with challenges. They departed from their Bizkaian villages, and though almost all left with the intention of returning in several years, they often said good-bye to parents, siblings, and friends that they would never see again. They traveled by train to ports in Bilbao or Le Havre, France, or by boat to Liverpool, England. They crossed the Atlantic by steamship, at times alone or in small groups, sometimes meeting fellow Bizkaians en route. The transatlantic voyage usually took anywhere from seven to thirteen days, and conditions were quite uncomfortable—crowded quarters, awful odors, no privacy, and the incessant rocking of the ship, which left many passengers moaning from seasickness. One Basque who crossed the Atlantic early in the century recalled that the turbulence was so bad during the thirteen-day journey that almost all passengers became seasick, and two eventually died on board. The steamship that Juan Achabal was taking to New York in 1893 sank in the middle of the Atlantic; a passing ship picked up the survivors and delivered them to Galveston, Texas. Achabal survived but lost all his possessions except the clothes he wore, and he still had to get from Texas to Boise.[3]

Arriving at American entry points such as Castle Garden or Ellis Island could be just as dreadful as the ocean journey. Carrying all their possessions with them and hoping that they would not be lost or stolen, the immigrants queued up, waiting for officials to spit out questions about their health, their financial situation, their politics. Many in these lines lost their family name or had it radically altered as officials struggled to record the unfamiliar names and spellings. Doctors poked and probed them in search of fleas, lice, and the contagious eye disease trachoma. Immigrants hoped they would not receive a chalked letter on their clothing (*L* for lung problem, *H* for heart disease, *X* for mental sickness); if they did, it meant they would be subject to further tests and possible deportation. Lucy Garatea, who early in the century immigrated to Idaho at age fifteen, had to spend eleven days on Ellis Island, sleeping each night on a bench with only one blanket and a little pillow, while officials further investigated her immigration application. Although 98 percent of immigrants went through Ellis Island without any problems, there were many cases of individuals who were sent back or families who were separated because one member was refused entry.[4]

Basques represented only a tiny portion of all immigrants. In the immigration lines they encountered languages and people from all over the world—an astounding experience for them, since they had just barely left the homogeneous setting of their village. Once through the gates, however, many early Basques immigrating to Idaho would hear the familiar sound of their native language rising above the din of dozens of others. In the 1890s one Basque man, Valentin Aguirre, founded a boardinghouse in New York, the Casa Vizcaína, and later added a travel agency to help immigrants get across the country. Regina Bastida, age sixteen when she emigrated from Ondarroa, Bizkaia, remembered staying at the Casa Vizcaína in 1920 on her way to Idaho. Valentin Aguirre or one of his agents, she said, "met all the boats and exchanged the money and explained the problems and took care of all the Basque people that came into New York." At Aguirre's hotel they could eat familiar food, exchange stories in Euskera with fellow travelers, and rest after the exhausting journey. Valentin Aguirre helped Basques find work or book train tickets to the West, often pinning cards on their jackets that would identify their destination for the conductor.[5]

The train trips from the East Coast to Idaho were not without their own anecdotes, most of them involving the unending source of frustration for all non-English-speaking immigrants—their inability to communicate. There is the story about the young Basque man whose three-word English vocabulary—"ham-and-eggs"—determined his menu for the entire trip across the country. Another Basque, warned by his mother to keep his faith in the libertine United States, wrote to tell her not to worry: he had seen people on the train to Idaho moving their lips as they prayed the Rosary, the same way women did at his hometown church. He later learned that the Americans were chewing gum; he had never seen it before. One author wrote that Basque immigrants would often pack a string of pungent chorizo along with them, which when "tossed over the back of a young Basque . . . must have made quite a hit with his fellow travelers."[6]

Crossing the United States, young Basques experienced dozens of "firsts": their first encounter with people of other races, their first train transfer, the first of their many awful struggles with English. Accustomed to spending months without leaving the sloping isolation of the farm, many were awed and bewildered by the distance of the trek, with endless stretches of flat farmland speeding by. As their trains entered Idaho, the sight of their new home contrasted sharply with their visions of the promised land they had anticipated. They had come from a region where cold winds blowing off the ocean would bring more than forty inches of precipitation every year, where their sheets were always cold and damp from the humidity. Although the Basque Country, resting at the western edge of the Pyrenees Mountains, and Idaho, on the western edge of the Rocky Mountains, both have high peaks, the geographical similarities end there. Most of the area in southern Idaho was sagebrush plain that receives around ten inches of precipitation a year. At the turn of the century, much of the southern Idaho land, interrupted only by trees bordering the Boise, Payette, and Snake Rivers, had yet to be cultivated into farmland.[7]

While the geography may have been different, those who took the branch rail line into Boise might have seen a hint of the wealth they aspired to. At the turn of the century, Boise's population had doubled from a decade earlier, and by 1910 it would approach twenty thousand. When the earliest Basque immigrants arrived at the Oregon Short Line depot on Front Street, often met by employers, they stepped out into a growing town: four- and five-story sandstone office buildings rose above older two-story wooden shops. By 1900 the French chateau Idanha Hotel was completed, the first of several six-story buildings to come. The immigrants, often wearing the same suit they had been wearing the day they left Europe weeks earlier, might have had an opportunity to stroll on the new concrete sidewalks and watch electric trolley cars roll by on streets that had only begun to be paved in 1897. They could venture through a small Chinatown or a red-light district called Levi's Alley.[8]

These Basque immigrants might have wandered onto Grove Street, the poplar-lined avenue one block south of Main Street, where Boise's elite had been building mansions since the town's incorporation in 1866. Later, Basque boardinghouses were established in this area—places where many Basque parties would be held, where Basques would eat lavish Christmas dinners and dance out of the dining room and into the street. In these houses they would form lasting friendships and sometimes even meet the women who became their wives. Their children and grandchildren would build a Basque Center here, start a Basque pub, organize Basque dances and dinners. But to a young Basque immigrant arriving around 1900—poor, homesick, baffled by the new surroundings—such thoughts probably never occurred.[9]

Getting Established

"This is a sad country to live in forever," one young Basque man wrote to a friend shortly after arriving in Idaho early in the century, but "it's good for earning a little money for a few years to return to Spain, to be rich and look for a girlfriend."[10] Though they were lonely in this distant, strange area of southern Idaho, they expected their misery to be temporary, to be endured only until they accumulated enough money to be comfortable back home. Still, during their entry, this thought rarely was enough to console them. Years later, one woman would say that before she immigrated, she had an image of a wealthy America with "rich people golfing." But after her first discouraging days in Idaho, that image was shattered. "I couldn't believe it," she said. "I wondered why I came."[11]

Fellow Basques in the state helped ease this adjustment. By the turn of the century the small pocket of Basques in Boise and other towns in southern Idaho had begun to open rooming houses for the new immigrants, places where newcomers could find familiar language and pursue job possibilities. Other immigrants were fortunate enough to enter the country with help from friends and relatives. Of fifty-three Basques headed for Boise from 1897 to 1902, almost half claimed to have relatives or acquaintances already living in the United States. In 1902 sixteen-year-old Marcelino Aldecoa followed his brother Domingo Aldecoa, who had come to Boise in 1899 also at the age of sixteen. Boise's 1909 directory has seven listings with the Basque surname Gabiola, five with Goicoechea. Miguel Gabica had five siblings in Idaho by 1917.[12]

This chain migration meant that the Basque communities that dotted the West were populated by immigrants who came not only from the same region but often from the same area within it. In the Monterey–San Francisco area of California most of the Basques came from the Navarrese village of Echalar. In Buffalo, Wyoming, the common denominator was not even a region but an individual, Jean Esponda of Saint-Etienne-de-Baigorri, the initial settler of that community. The overwhelming majority of Basques who settled in Idaho came from the same small region within Bizkaia—roughly from the coastal towns of Bermeo to the west and Ondarroa to the east and inland of these boundaries no more than twenty kilometers. The source of the immigrants may be even further narrowed down; Silen's study indicates that

44 percent came from the five coastal villages of Ea, Bedarona, Ispaster, Lekeitio, and Mendexa.[13]

Family and Old Country ties connected the new immigrants to Idaho's sheep industry with the sponsorship of successful pioneer Basques. The industry was a latecomer to Idaho, which, before statehood, had been a thoroughfare for migrating flocks. After the expansion of railroads in the 1880s, however, the industry boomed in the state, and early sheepmen like Frank Gooding and John Hailey began to make fortunes. In 1890 there were 614,000 head of sheep in the state, by 1900 almost 2.1 million. Basques like José Bengoechea and Juan Achabal were part of this boom, building the basis for flocks that would become some of the largest in the American West.[14]

Still, young Basque men were getting involved in an industry that was hardly glorified by American society. Despite the potential wealth it offered, sheepherding carried a stigma. Sheepherders were "outcasts and ne'er-do-wells, shifty characters too undependable to be hired in the mines or by cattlemen." One author noted that the sheepherder, the once-honorable figure of the pastoral ages, now "has only one consolation left, and that is the secure knowledge that he is working on rock bottom." One could not fire a shotgun into a crowd in the West, he added, without hitting somebody who had herded sheep, "but it would probably take the charge in the other barrel to make him admit it." Low regard for the sheepherder, coupled with the Basques' short-term profit plan, inspired much of the early scorn that the immigrants faced in the state.[15]

To add to their difficulties, most Basque immigrants brought with them no sheepherding experience. If they had herded sheep at all back home, it was with small bands that provided cheese and wool for the family, a situation that involved none of the loneliness, financial risk, or danger of the large-scale herding in Idaho. These inexperienced herders had to learn quickly, often within days of arriving in Idaho, how to herd up to 2,500 head of sheep by themselves. They had to grow accustomed to the bloody, messy work of the lambing season from January to mid-March, when they would help deliver thousands of lambs and form bands. They had to learn how to shear the sheep in March and April and move them to the foothills to feed on the spring grasses in May. During the summer, herders drove the bands up the mountains, following the retreating line of snow, steering them from one meadow to another, descending only to ship the lambs in July. They began to trail down to the valleys in October before the first snowfall, and by December the sheep were in the corral. Herders would then begin to prepare for the birth of the first lambs, and the process would start again.[16]

Although held in low regard by most Americans, sheepherding offered one of the few passages for Basques to the United States; it was the only alternative for a young man with few skills and no knowledge of English. As one immigrant claimed, "The worst is no can talk." The only advantages they brought were their agrarian background and their capacity for hard work, qualities that were quickly noticed by Idaho sheep ranchers. Though they had little sheepherding experience, almost all the immigrants had toiled for years back in Bizkaia on dizzying slopes in all weather, and they could endure almost any physical challenge.[17]

They would learn, however, that often the hardest challenges of sheepherding were not physical, but mental and emotional. Most of them found that the worst part of herding was the loneliness and isolation, especially in the summer when herders would go for weeks without seeing another human being. Sabino Landa, who had never herded sheep before coming to the United States in 1920, found himself all alone in the Idaho hills with more than a thousand head of sheep. "I was so homesick," he said. "I've never been alone like that. I cry all day and all night." After an agonizing week alone, he finally saw a man approaching and was elated after hearing him shout, "Gazte!" [Youngster!]: "I jump four feet when I heard that." Accompanied only by a dog and the constantly bleating sheep, with occasional visits from a camptender delivering supplies, Basque herders were tortured by loneliness for weeks. "I remember when I got the first letter from my mother," one Basque herder said. "I had to go behind the tree to read it because I was crying like a baby." Hours and hours spent thinking the same thoughts— about home, what they were missing, their responsibilities—overpowered some, and they would have to return to the Basque Country having made no money and losing their family's travel investment.[18]

In extreme cases, the isolation created an "occupational hazard"—insanity. The herders called it being "sheeped" or "sage-brushed." Later, when Basques in Boise formed a health insurance organization, part of its coverage included return passage to the Basque Country for any member who suffered from mental illness. In 1908 a Basque herder in

Mountain Home was tried in court to determine if there was cause to place him in a mental institution. After hearing the results of his examination by a local doctor, the court declared, "He was so far disordered in mind as to endanger health, person and property," and he was committed to an institution in Blackfoot.[19]

Mortal dangers abounded, both to themselves and to their flocks, from lightning to snakebite. The sheep could acquire spotted fever from ticks or get stuck in the snow and freeze, always a threat for neophyte herders. One herder wrote home in 1918 to say he had been lucky to lose only 40 sheep in a snowstorm; another herder had lost 1,500. During the summer months in the mountain meadows, the sheep were susceptible to attacks by coyotes, cougars, or bears. If the herders lost the sheep, they lost their jobs and might have difficulty finding work with another sheep outfit. Even worse, if they injured themselves, there was nobody to help them get back to camp.[20]

The country they passed through, barely changed from frontier times, presented challenges that a young man from the Basque Country could not have been prepared for. One herder suffered a shock when a group of Native Americans approached his camp. Alone, unsure what to do, he opted for a peaceful solution: he offered them coffee. Though they did not harm him, they did frighten him. Not knowing much more English than the herder, they told him, "You are no good." The herder was a bit relieved when he found out they were referring to the coffee.[21]

More severe disputes developed from the controversy over grazing land. As Basques drove flocks from the desert wintering grounds to the mountain pastures for the summer, they encountered cowboys grazing their cattle in the same areas. In 1872 the Idaho territorial legislature passed a bill preventing herders from grazing their sheep within two miles of "any human habitation and any cattle range," greatly restricting herders' grazing rights. The bill was clearly intended to drive away migrating flocks of sheep. Though in theory itinerant herders had as much legal right to public land as established ranchers, cattlemen traditionally had shared it only among themselves. Idaho's early courts supported the cattle industry. One justice wrote in 1902: "Sheep eat the herbage closer to the ground than cattle or horses do, and, their hooves being sharp, they devastate and kill the growing vegetation wherever they graze for any considerable time." He added, "It is a matter of common experience that a large band of sheep to the windward, affects one's sense of smell when a considerable distance away."[22]

The herders, unable to communicate well, had to confront the cowboys alone. Some sheep and cattle disputes were settled in court, others by violence. Records from the 1911 case *State of Idaho v. Luis Yturaspe* report that James A. Percy sent his dogs to scatter four Basque sheep bands; later, he chased one of the herders, Luis Yturaspe, with a hammer. Percy charged that Yturaspe then pulled a gun on him. In 1911 cattleman Harry Hoyt brought assault charges against a Basque herder, claiming that he had asked the herder to remove 2,500 lambs from his property near Boise. When Hoyt began to drive the sheep away, the herder fired his rifle in the air and, according to court records, mustered enough English to say, "Stop you son of a bitch or I will shoot you." The herder was fined five hundred dollars.[23]

In 1917 a land dispute involving a Basque herder even reached the United States Supreme Court. In *Omaechevarria v. State of Idaho,* the state's highest court had upheld the law keeping herds of sheep two miles from any cattle range, saying "segregation is essential to protect the cattle industry and prevent serious breaches of the peace between cattlemen and sheepmen." The United States Supreme Court affirmed the decision. In the Court's opinion, Justice Louis Brandeis wrote: "It is not an arbitrary discrimination to give preference to cattle owners in prior occupancy. . . . For experience shows that sheep do not require protection against encroachment by cattle, and that cattle rangers are not likely to encroach upon ranges previously occupied by sheep herders."[24]

Idaho cattlemen saw these Basque herders as selfish nomads who wanted to exploit every inch of grazing land and as tightfisted foreigners who niggled over every penny to create fortunes that they would ship out of the country. Eventually the criticism spread to other sectors of society. The National Wool Growers in 1918 condemned "alien sheepmen" for ruining public grazing land and returning to their countries. "No one ought to be able to use the public land unless he is a citizen of the United States." A 1909 article in the *Caldwell Tribune* was more direct: "The sheepmen of Owyhee county are sorely beset by Biscayans [Bizkaians] . . . and trouble may result most any time." It blamed the problem on the greed of the sheepmen, because "they, themselves introduced the Biscayans [Bizkaians] into the country and instructed them in the sheep business, because they could get them for a smaller wage." The business practices and culture of "the Bascos are on par with those of the Chinaman," but the *Tribune* added that the "Chinaman" was not "filthy, treacherous and meddlesome" like the Basques. Basques were "clannish and undesirable," and unless something was done, they would "make life impossible for the white man."[25]

Their lack of familiarity with English, which, given their isolation as herders, was hard to correct, also made them targets for prejudice or exploitation by their American bosses. One Basque said this problem was especially apparent at payment time. The herder, expecting a full year's salary, would sometimes be told that his company had had a bad year. "So, after you been in the hills for nine or ten months, they tell you they can't pay you." Most forms of prejudice came through small scuffles or verbal insults when Basques would be called "dirty black Basco," a pejorative term similar to "wop" or "wetback." Some prejudice was demonstrated during the Spanish-American War, when Idahoans still lumped Basques together with Spaniards. Antonio Azcuenaga, arriving at his blacksmith shop in Jordan Valley one morning, found a Spanish flag hung in his doorway, indicating that the shop was not to be patronized.[26]

The young Basques who came to Idaho in the first years of the twentieth century had to endure these challenges, sometimes for the survival of their family back home but also to earn respect from the community. "It was unthinkable," one author stated, "that a Basque emigrant could return to his village without having succeeded in his immigration efforts." After eight years in Idaho, one herder reported to his father that he had not made enough money yet to return to the Basque Country; he might be seen around his native village with "holes in [his] pants" and people would call him the "Bad American."[27]

It was this drive that partially explains the success of the Basques in Idaho. Many herders relished the competition to see who could bring in the heaviest lambs. Andy Little, one of the state's most prominent sheepmen, hired Basques throughout his life. His biographer wrote: "The Littles are the first to say that Basque herders, managers, foremen and other employees helped build Andy's business as much as anyone."[28]

Basques also became known for their loyalty. After thirty-five years of herding, one Basque was beginning to wear down, and his eyesight was failing him. He suggested to his employer that he should pay him off and he would leave. His employer, fond of the herder and grateful for his decades of loyalty, teased him sarcastically: "I always knew that you Basques couldn't be depended upon," he said. "Here today and gone tomorrow, jumping around from one job to the other." The herder stood silent in front of his boss, twisting his hat in his thick, weathered, calloused hands, and with a determined look said, "I'm no quitter. I can't see so good anymore, I can't work so good anymore; but, if you want, I stay."[29]

Their salaries were low, usually no more than forty dollars a month, but that was a princely sum in the Basque Country, where wages averaged around fifty pesetas a month, just a few dollars. They tried to save every cent. One young Basque, writing to his father in December 1915, said he planned to go to Boise for a few days, but he would not stay for Christmas because he would spend too much money. They were known in the industry as being frugal or, by more unkind critics, miserly. Long-time secretary of state Pete Cenarrusa remembered a Basque herder who used string from gunnysacks to repair his pants rather than buy thread.[30] To save money, Juan Achabal waited until other workers had thrown away their blood-covered overalls after lambing season; he then retrieved them, washed them, and sold them to other herders.

Basques were gaining a reputation as "the irreplaceable backbone of the open-range, transhumant sheep outfits in the American West." Their frugality and sacrifice allowed them to fulfill their dreams of success. José Bengoechea was now "Joe" Bengoechea, no longer a simple herder but the owner of thousands of head of sheep. He came to the United States in 1889, and after working in California and Nevada he settled in Idaho, where he was able to buy his own bands of sheep after only three years in the United States. By 1910 he owned extensive property in Mountain Home and built the landmark Mountain Home Hotel, which still stands.[31]

Juan Achabal, now John Archabal, was even more successful and influential. By developing an early profit-sharing system, he initiated a way to reward loyalty from herders and provide even more financial incentive for them. The herders could take part of their wages in lambs and tend them along with the company's band. With his own interest at stake, the employee would be even more conscientious and, over several years, would build up larger flocks. Over the course of his career, Archabal employed hundreds of Basque herders in this fashion. Others followed suit, and the practice provided opportunity for many other friends and family members from the Old Country.

Bengoechea and Archabal were living examples of the American dream. They became some of the largest sheep owners in Oregon and Idaho, and their success spread to their home villages and fueled the dreams of impressionable youth who wanted more than what they had. In 1925 Archabal bought a brand-new car in Detroit, had it shipped to Europe, and drove it around the Basque Country, where he hosted large dinners for family and friends. In a country where oxen and donkeys were still commonplace, one can only imagine the attention that Archabal drew. Children ran alongside the car, touching it, and helping to polish it—many no doubt dreaming of the day when they would be behind the wheel of their own car.[32]

Successful experiences like these gave those who braved the barriers of America a sense of confidence and independence. "[Sheepherding] makes you self-sufficient," a Basque immigrant said. "You learn to survive no matter what. Even if a snake bites you, you say, 'I gotta make it on my own.' You know that nobody else is going to help you, your mother is not going to be kissing you." Some went back to the Basque Country and made a better life for themselves. Others found that despite their dreams of returning to the Basque Country, something unexpected had happened. They realized that they had changed and that their home and future were now in America.[33]

3

Boardinghouses:
The Closest Thing to Home

By 1910 it became apparent that some Basques had abandoned their original plans to return to the Basque Country and decided to make their stay in Idaho permanent. Several of the first group of immigrants even filed for American citizenship; in Ada County from 1906 to 1909 at least forty-eight Basques filed for citizenship, possibly in response to the criticism that they were hoarding money and taking it out of the country. From 1888 to 1903 only thirteen Basques filed Declarations of Intention.[1]

Although the majority chose not to naturalize, they were settling throughout southern Idaho and eastern Oregon, wherever the sheep industry had scattered them. Eventually Basques were widespread in the area straddling the Oregon border into Jordan Valley and Ontario, through Caldwell and Nampa, to the desert of Elmore County, to Gooding, Jerome, Shoshone, Twin Falls, north to Hailey and Ketchum, in the valleys below the Sawtooth Mountains, all the way east across the state to Pocatello. In 1910 Boise was on its way to becoming, as one author suggested, "the Basque center of the Northwest," with almost five hundred Basques out of a total population of twenty thousand.[2]

To make the transition from migrant to permanent resident, Basques had to solve practical problems, not the least of which was staying employed. The sheep industry, with its variable financial returns, seasonal nature, and labor gluts and shortages, often left them unemployed for months out of the year. They needed some kind of safety net—at the very least, a place to stay while they searched for work. Though they had little or no English, they still had to receive medical attention, buy clothing, send money to their families, and acquire the everyday things they needed for their new lives.

Beyond these practical concerns, even the toughest and most determined herders missed home and craved Basque companionship. They hungered for news from home, but letters were rare, often arriving months after they were sent. One letter sent from Bizkaia on June 23, 1912, was received in Idaho on October 9, 1912. At holiday time, their homesickness and longing for companionship became more acute. One herder wrote home, "Make sure to buy good fish and wine because Christmas only happens once a year. And Christmas is for people to enjoy. At least, for those who can." Later he continued, "Have a good Christmas. I'm planning on spending it with the sheep." The herders' loneliness also meant they were ripe for romance. Basque herders throughout the West left thousands of carvings on aspen trees, many of them crude outlines of female figures or messages of sexual fantasy. Isolated by the sheep industry, they had few encounters with women, and their linguistic shortcomings were a hindrance in the courting of American women.[3]

One of the most important institutions in the Basque-American experience, the boardinghouse, grew out of these needs. For young Basque immigrants a long way from home, the boardinghouses became "the village church, the town tavern, the bank and the health dispensary." The boardinghouses allowed them to undertake their first forays into American culture and simultaneously form small Basque enclaves in towns throughout Idaho, which served as "safe havens" of retreat from American society. Sheepherding helped Basques get started in Idaho, but boardinghouses helped keep them there.[4]

The boardinghouses originated as rooming houses in the 1890s, with established Basque families renting out a bedroom to a newly arrived immigrant. Young Basques had "barely a ticket to come to United States," a Shoshone Basque said. "And then they were here and had no home. Where would they go? To hotel, when they didn't know nobody, they have no language?" They needed a place "where they got language. . . . So [a Basque] that had one extra room took one in. Two extra rooms, two men. That's the way boardinghouses started. It's a helping hand, that's what they were really, a helping hand."[5]

If a Basque couple could afford it, they expanded to several rooms, or bought a building and became hotel keepers exclusively. In 1900 Juan and Teresa Yribar opened a boardinghouse at 118 South Seventh Street in Boise, within view of the old domeless capitol and around the block from the town's most important bars and restaurants on Main Street. José Uberuaga opened the City Lodging House in 1901. Around 1915 Francisco and Gabina Aguirre bought the Star Hotel from José and Felipa Uberuaga and ran a boardinghouse and shoe repair shop for decades. Mirroring the growth in the Basque population in the state, boardinghouses started small but quickly proliferated in response to the demand. In 1920 Francisco and Florentina Sabala established the first Basque boardinghouse in Twin Falls. Shoshone had the Berriochoa Boardinghouse, the Beitia'a Boardinghouse, and the pool hall. Near the railroad station in Gooding, Claudio Ascuena built the Casa Española boardinghouse in 1907 with twelve bedrooms and a large kitchen, the only room in the house with running water. Hailey sported two rooming houses, the Rialto Hotel and Bar, and the Inchausti Boardinghouse (also known as the Gem House). Nampa had the Spanish Hotel and the Modern Hotel, Burns had the Star Hotel and the Plaza Hotel. The boardinghouse idea spread north to Mullan, where Dominica Soloaga Mingo operated a boardinghouse from 1925 to 1929 to accommodate a group of Basques working in the nearby mines.[6]

In 1910 there were at least six Basque boardinghouses listed in the Boise directory, and more were to come. They were within a few blocks of each other, mostly on Idaho or Grove Streets, a short walk from the old Front Street train depot where new Basques were arriving steadily. In 1912 at least 238 young Basques were listed as part-time residents at the Modern Rooming House at 613^{1}/2 West Idaho, and forty-three others were at the DeLamar Rooming House on Grove Street, the beautiful mansion built by banker C. W. Moore in 1879 and converted into a boardinghouse by Antonio Letemendi. Herders would begin to stream in by late fall as the herding industry took its seasonal pause, and the groups coming to stay, as one owner remembered, "got bigger and bigger and bigger, and then just before Christmas, here comes the whole crew."[7]

After months of being exposed to the elements—from the hottest days in August to the first snows in late fall—eating hundreds of the same monotonous meals of stew or beans that they had prepared them-

44

selves, sleeping on lumpy cots in wagons or on the ground, the herders relished eating civilized food and resting in real beds with heavy quilts—and no sheep bleating in the background. For about one dollar a day they ate as well as or better than they had as children in the Basque Country, crowded around tables with the owner's family or, in the larger boardinghouses, elbow to elbow with other herders on break. The meals were usually served family-style and in large quantity. They ate in courses beginning with beans, then soup or salad, often prepared with fresh vegetables delivered that morning by Chinese farmers. The main course usually included a roast, chicken, tongue, fish, and chorizos that many boardinghouses made from scratch. All of these were mopped up with fresh bread and accompanied by red wine, which, if not as smooth as the wine back home, was much better than what they had on the open range. The boardinghouses became more than a place to stay for the herders: "For us, it was heaven . . . the closest thing to home," one Basque recalled.[8]

The herders would sleep late, sometimes getting up barely in time for lunch. Early boardinghouses had no central heating, and the herders would stay warm in their beds or drift down to the dining room to gather by the potbellied stove or fireplace, or play card games like poker or *mus* (the traditional Basque game that pits two teams of two players against each other), bluffing, shouting, and pounding their way to forty points. Most important, they had the opportunity to talk, and they talked for hours—about home, about herding, about their strange new surroundings, about anything, to anybody who would listen. They had seen few people the previous eleven months, and they had a lot to say. Nicasio "Nick" Beristain remembered waking up at his boardinghouse in Boise and going downstairs for breakfast, often to be eagerly greeted by a herder fresh from the range. "I wanted to eat my breakfast, but hell, they didn't want to eat. They got all [the food] they wanted up in the hills. They just wanted to talk—for them it was food. I knew why, I went through the same thing."[9]

In the evenings the air would fill up with conversation and thick cigar smoke, the trademark of boardinghouses, as the boarders lingered over their coffee, brandy, or cognac, or idled on the front steps when the weather was warm enough. On the porch of 607 Grove Street in Boise, the address of what used to be Uberuaga's Boardinghouse, one can still see hundreds of scrapes on the red brick walls where the boarders would strike their wooden matches to light their cigars for the long conversations ahead.

Something to Fall Back On

For those who were temporarily laid off, boardinghouse loitering was not only recreational but also practical as they awaited news about jobs. Boardinghouse owners were often generous about extending credit, and Basque hotels became unofficial employment agencies. More Basques were immigrating, and more boardinghouses were opening. In Nampa there was the Spanish Hotel on Twelfth Avenue, run by Tomas and Tomasa Jausoro; in 1920, Francisco and Florentina Sabala opened the first boardinghouse in Twin Falls; Santa Bilbao also established a Basque hotel there after operating several in Boise, Jordan Valley, and Jerome. Sheepmen knew that when they were short of labor during periods like the winter lambing season, they could almost always go the boardinghouses to find reliable employees among those playing cards or resting.[10]

The recruiting, however, was not confined to sheepmen; Basques would often find employment on farms, in mines, or with construction projects, which would provide them a coveted opportunity to leave sheepherding temporarily, if not for good. In Boise many found work constructing the Arrowrock Dam (the highest dam in the world when it was completed in 1916), and teams of Basque men were employed in the sandstone quarries around town. It offered young Basques their first leap from herding, a change that, for most, was eagerly anticipated. They could remain in town, possibly earn more money, and stay at the boardinghouses, where the cooks would pack their lunches. The system worked well for everyone: the immigrants got jobs, the businesses got cheap labor, and the boardinghouse owners got year-round, steady business.[11]

For the boardinghouse owners, however, steady business also meant long days. The boarders, some of whom showed up unannounced and penniless, needed constant attention from the moment they arrived. Owners often met new immigrants at the train station and escorted them to their hotels. John Anduiza remembered that when a new herder found a job, his father "would take them down to Pioneer Tent Company and get them all set up with their bedding and everything." They needed warm jackets, boots, work pants, and supplies they had not brought with them. The owners, often former herders themselves, were familiar with what the business required. Because most young Basques arrived broke, owners extended credit for their supplies and their stay at the boardinghouse, and the herders would pay them back after receiving their first check. By the time they established a hotel, most owners had acquired a passable command of English, a skill that aided newcomers immensely. If Basque immigrants wanted to buy clothes or medicine, open a bank account, or, perhaps most important, send a cashier's check to their families in Europe, the owner would escort them to the bank and translate for them. John Anduiza recalled his father, "Big Jack" Anduiza, taking herders to the bank after they had been paid. After working a full year for this payment, many, especially the younger, more naïve ones, would be eager to spend some of it. Knowing that their families might be depending for survival on the checks they sent, Big Jack would put the money in an account under his own name, telling the herders, "When you want it, come and see me."[12]

The boardinghouses, again serving a practical need, provided a home base for their boarders, especially the sheepherders, who for most of the year were roaming the hills and could not contact their families. They would receive mail from home at their boardinghouse address. (One herder told his family he could be reached at "Grobe S.t. 1107" in "Norte America Boise Ydaho.") Other Basques received letters addressed to "Boise, Idaho, California." Owners also provided year-round storage space for their boarders, who sometimes would find their suits cleaned and pressed a year or more after they had left them in mothballs in the attic.[13]

If a herder was sick or suffered an accident, he could come in from the hills for treatment at a boardinghouse, where doctors often made calls. Early in the century the doctor in Gooding treated many of his patients at the Casa Española, because the town did not yet have a hospital. Dr. Robert S. Smith recalled making regular visits to hotels in downtown Boise, especially in the winter months, "when they seemed unusually susceptible to respiratory infections." Basques could recuperate in the boardinghouses, mend bones broken in construction accidents, sweat out intense fevers contracted at sheep camps, or fight, and sometimes lose, battles with pneumonia. On happier occasions, doctors would rush to boardinghouses to deliver babies. Henry Alegria, whose family moved to Boise from Bizkaia in 1911, insisted that more babies were born at Juan Yribar's boardinghouse, which was open from 1900 to 1935, than any other place in Boise, "outside of St. Luke's Hospital."[14]

The medical bills could present a problem for new Basque immigrants who were kept out of work for weeks and months while they recuperated. Estacio "Stack" Yribar, who grew up in his parents' boardinghouse in Boise, said, "Herders didn't have any insurance. They never had anything to fall back on in case they got sick. In the old days, when someone got sick, they just used to pass the hat around."[15]

Early in the century Basques saw the need to establish a more formal response to medical emergencies. In 1908, largely from the impetus of Big Jack Anduiza, a group established La Sociedad de Socorros Mutuos (Society of Mutual Security). Open to Spanish and Basque males, the society quickly grew to about two hundred members. Once they paid their dues, originally ten dollars a year with a two-dollar entry fee, members would receive complete medical coverage, a daily stipend when unable to work, and even insurance for funeral expenses. The society also paid the passage back to the Basque Country for any member who became permanently disabled in an accident or mentally disturbed from herding sheep. Between 1908 and 1960 the association's 1,050 members received $425,000 in aid. In later years, similar Basque insurance groups for women were formed—La Fraternidad Vasca Americana and La Organisación Independiente Sociale. The insurance societies became a savior for many Basque immigrants.[16]

In 1918, however, the Socorros Mutuos's resources were nearly exhausted by the Spanish flu epidemic, which struck worldwide. The epidemic forced the organization to raise extra money for treatment or burial of Basque victims, including those who had never joined the organization. Many Idaho Basques died from the flu, among them the family of Boni Oyarzabal, a sheepherder near Mountain Home. When he discovered that his wife and young child had contracted the flu, he attempted to get them across the desert and find a doctor, but they did not make it. Friends found Boni delirious and his wife and child dead in the back of the wagon. A section of the Mountain Home cemetery dedicated to those who perished in 1918 attests to the fact that the Oyarzabals were not the only ones who suffered. In Boise dozens of Basques contracted influenza and died. Henry Alegria of Boise recalled that his brother Charlie became sick in November 1918. Every day for two weeks he visited Charlie at St. Alphonsus Hospital, finding him "in the hallway, walking around in his bathrobe." Then things apparently took a turn for the better, and one day Charlie told Henry he would be getting out of the hospital the next morning and that Henry should bring him his street clothes. After work the next day, Henry recalled, "I went to [Charlie's] rooming house, 613 West Idaho, for his things. That's when I learned of his death." The day of Charlie's funeral, five other Basque victims were buried. Henry attended all six funerals, and another brother, Felix, was an altar server at five of them. An older Basque man, seeing how tired Felix was, sent him home before the sixth, his brother Charlie's.[17]

Women Do the Dirty Work

"Work, work, work—you know—work, work, work—that's all—work, work." This was not a Basque sheepherder's recollection of his life; it was the refrain of a Basque woman speaking of her average day as a sixteen-year-old boardinghouse maid. From the time boardinghouses were built, they provided a means for hundreds of Basque women to immigrate to the United States. Before the boardinghouses, the only female immigrants were wives or fiancées of Basque men who had established enough financial security to buy a house and start a business. The 1900 U.S. Census recorded only five Basque females in Idaho. But just as sheepherding offered a way for men to immigrate, the boardinghouses began to pull young single women from Bizkaia to work as domestics. Paralleling the men's experience, in many cases the women's plans to stay only temporarily were swept away by unanticipated events.[18]

It would be difficult to overemphasize the importance of Basque women to the boardinghouses, and thus to the development of Idaho's Basque community. One elderly Basque woman sighed and said, "What women in those days didn't go through." Juanita "Jay" Hormaechea, who was born in 1908 at a boardinghouse on Sixth Street and later worked at several in downtown Boise, said Basque women, even those not employed in boardinghouses, were the cement that held the Basque community in Idaho together. Punctuating her words with her forefinger, Jay said, "They rarely got any recognition for their efforts, but you've

got to give them credit for the work they did to keep their homes together, their children together. Without them this community would
have never made it."[19]

Single Basque women who immigrated early in the century came to
America much as the men had, as "economic refugees" who had heard
about jobs from friends or relatives. Life in the Basque Country offered
women even fewer alternatives than men: marriage with the inheritor
of a farm, entrance to a convent, or employment as a maid in Bilbao,
where they would earn ten pesetas a month. But the American West,
with its expanding network of boardinghouses that needed Basque-
speaking labor, provided them another option. Basque newspapers ad-
vertised positions as domestic helpers in private homes or in rooming
houses; owners would front the cost of the trip, usually to be repaid out
of the woman's wages. In the 1920s Francisco and Gabina Aguirre needed
help at the Star Rooming House on Idaho Street in Boise; besides running the rooming house, Francisco, known as Zapatero (Spanish for
"shoemaker"), was busy with his shoe store, which was in the front of
the building. So Gabina wrote to her sister in Lekeitio, Bizkaia, to ask if
she would send her daughter to work as a maid. The daughter, Lucy
Garatea, said, "I didn't want to come! I didn't want to come!" But at age
fifteen, she did come—and she wouldn't return to the Basque Country
for thirty-three years.[20]

Years later, Lucy could still recall her aunt's voice jolting her from the
warmth of her bed at seven in the morning to start the day. "Ez, tía, ez!"
[No, aunt, no! in Basque and Spanish], Lucy pleaded, hoping for more
sleep and a break from the constant work at the boardinghouse. "On
Monday, we washed the clothes; I spent the whole day over the sink,
washing and washing. On Tuesday, I ironed. Wednesday, we scrubbed
all the floors *belauniko* [on our knees]." She remembered each day as
more of the same routine, some days lasting until well past midnight as
she waited on sore feet for boarders to put out their cigars, drain their
last drinks, and sing the last song, signaling her chance to start picking
up dishes.[21]

Other women were more willing to make the journey. "I really
thought I could come to America and find me a rich boyfriend," said
one woman, who immigrated in 1920 to work at José Bengoechea's
Mountain Home Hotel. They soon discovered that their work was anything but glamorous; instead, it was often more exhausting than labor

on the family *baserri* had been. "Women had to do all the dirty work: scrub the floors, clean the toilets," Jay Hormaechea said. Boardinghouse women became machines, laboring long, monotonous day after long, monotonous day. Lacking many amenities, they relied on their own hands to finish their work. Women sent sheets to the nearby Chinese laundries, but the boarders' clothes were washed with a scrub board and dried on clotheslines in the summer or over stoves in the winter. When the herders left the boardinghouse for their annual migration, one former maid remembered, she would brush their suits and "clean their underwears." Hardwood floors had to be scrubbed by hand, and long splinters speared the women's knees. Marie Uriarte found an easier way to polish the floors at her Burns, Oregon, boardinghouse: She sat down on a dirty sheet yanked off a bed and had another maid pull her around the room.[22]

Years before heating and air-conditioning units, the extremes of both elements would hit the boardinghouses, windows crystallizing with frost in the winter, the air heavy with heat in the summer. One woman recalled her first boardinghouse winter in 1922. "It was terrible to work because it was ice-cold, and upstairs, I used to have to go into the bathroom and take off my shoes and stockings and put my feet in the hot water in the tub." On the bottom floor, however, there was a room with a potbellied stove where the men would play cards. "Boy, did I spend a lot of time there," she said.[23]

Women suffered the monotony of kitchen work in greasy, heavy air emanating from coal or wood stove ranges. Dishes and pots and pans had to be washed and dried, filled with food, then washed and dried again—three meals a day, every day. The women produced meals for twenty, thirty, forty. They had to shop almost every day for the cornucopia of food they would serve, and their first ventures into American society were made alone, often producing embarrassing results. In the grocery stores, Basque women, most of whom could not have asked for a glass of water in English upon their arrival in Idaho, were forced to seek out words like "bacon," "beef," "flour," "onion," "noodles," and dozens of others from their scanty vocabularies. One woman working in Mountain Home said she never knew how much money to hand over, so "I would give them a pile of money. I always went home with lots of change, and the guys at the boardinghouse would laugh." One morning the Mountain Home Hotel cook sent her to the butcher, and she assumed she could just point to what was needed as she always had. However, she did not see the item she needed inside the counter. After the butcher asked her what she wanted, she resorted to sign language: she stuck out her tongue. The confused butcher finally figured it out: "Oh, you would like some beef tongue," he said. Another Basque woman approached the butcher's counter and sheepishly began pointing to the joints on her elbow and knee. She finally gave up. She had forgotten how to say "soup bone."[24]

The elder women often took on roles that transcended the daily chores of putting food on the table and ironing boarders' shirts. They became "surrogate mothers," as one author described, easing the entry of young men into an indifferent world. As one herder recalled, "We didn't have no family or nothing, no mama mostly." He remembered going into his room at Letemendi's Boardinghouse on his birthday. It was his first away from home, and he started to cry. But Leandra Letemendi heard him. She went into the room and consoled him.[25]

New Reasons to Stay

For the young male boarders, most of whom had gone long stretches without seeing a single female, boardinghouses provided an opportunity to meet and converse with females from the Basque Country, or with the daughters of owners who were able to speak Basque. This produced a high rate of turnover among boardinghouse maids, because most married within months of arriving in Idaho. Boardinghouses, where young Basque couples met so frequently that they became known as "marriage mills," were even the site for some of their wedding receptions.[26]

The marriages often clinched the decisions of young Basques to stay in Idaho rather than return to the Basque Country. Regina Bastida, who had immigrated to Mountain Home with aspirations of marrying into wealth, met her husband, Juan, in a pool hall as he was completing his papers to return to the Basque Country. She had traveled to Boise to see her sister, whose husband owned the Merino Bar, and as she walked in she saw the room was "full of Basque guys, bunches of herders and everything. That is where I saw Juan." Later she said that she knew Juan was "sitting there and thinking, 'Here I am filling out papers to go back to Spain, and then in comes the girl I think I want to marry. I better stay here for a while.'" He proposed to her on their sixth date. Though she was initially unsure, "little by little getting married looked better than going back to the maid work," and she accepted. They were married in Boise in January 1921 and stayed in Idaho the rest of their lives, returning to the Basque Country only for brief visits.[27]

The occasions for many first meetings were festive dances and parties that boardinghouses threw. With the high ratio of men to women, competition for the women's company was keen. The boarders were usually in town for their one break of the year, the son of one owner remembered. "Around Christmastime especially, all of the herders were down from the hills, and they had about a month before they would have to go to lambing. Those were wild times, they'd come to town and really cut loose."[28]

The boardinghouses hosted impromptu dances in their dining rooms, and boarders would shove the tables to the side and dance to any music that was available. Herders who had mastered the accordion pumped out jotas, or someone would slide coin after coin into a nickelodeon. "We would dance and dance and dance," Lucy Garatea said. "One time this herder came in and put five dollars' worth of nickels in the player piano. 'Fuego!' [Fire!] We danced and danced. We were so young, you know."[29]

Except for the busy holiday season, dances were usually confined to Sundays, the only day off for most. Lucy Garatea, who received only room and board for her work, said she had only two hours off on Sunday. The young men she met in the Star Rooming House would offer to take her to movies at the Egyptian or Pinney theaters, to dances, to a show, "to Chinese [restaurants], all those things in two hours!" But after six and a half days of working, she said, "I think every time I went to a show I was sleeping."[30]

One woman claimed the only drawback to the boardinghouse dances was the "fresh" attitudes of some of the boarders, who had gone so long without female companionship. "When you worked in boardinghouses, you had to learn to fight the boys, because they got kind of smart and cocky, and their hands were . . ." Recent female arrivals from the Basque Country, she added, were often shocked by these bold advances; "those girls didn't know, but it didn't take them long to learn." One former maid said few of the boarders treated her roughly. "They probably knew better."[31]

Except for the occasional rude comment or advance, however, boardinghouses provided an excellent means for young Basque men and women to meet and begin a new life together in the United States. With young Basque women coming over more frequently, it became the norm to meet at a boardinghouse dinner or dance, a practice that contributed to the formation of Basque enclaves in Idaho. Among the immigrant generation, there was a very low rate of intermarriage with non-Basques. In one survey, only 5 of 119 Basques who immigrated to Idaho from 1889 to 1939 were married to non-Basques.[32]

4

Idahoans Get to Know the Basques

lthough Basques were becoming more drawn into these tight
communities clustered around the boardinghouses, they also
began to attract more attention from Idahoans. Outsiders
could stroll past boardinghouses and, struck by strange
notes from an accordion or the powerful aroma of leeks, wonder who
threw those parties that went on until far into the night. What place
was the source for these strange, unpronounceable names popping
up in town directories: Mendiola, Aldape, Basterechea, Guerricacheba-
rria, Urrutibeascoa, Arrizabalaga? Who were these Zubizarretas, these
Ybaibarriagas?

Many first noticed Basques through their sports. After 1910 Basques
could be heard shouting at their frontons, the courts where they played
the traditional sports *pelota,* handball, or *pala,* in which players strike a
hard leather-bound ball with thick wooden paddles. Frontons began to
spring up at the initiative of the boardinghouses. The first was built in
1910 in Boise by Domingo Zabala, who borrowed one thousand dollars
to construct its two walls, near what is now River Street. The same year
another fronton was constructed, on the west side of the newly built
Iberia Hotel on Ninth Street. The next year, in the spirit of competition
that arose between the boardinghouses, the Star Rooming House added
a court on its west side, covered with a canopy. By 1915 Anduiza's boardinghouse in Boise had built its indoor fronton, the longest in Idaho
and, according to one former player, "the best in the United States."

There were two in Mountain Home and another under construction in Jordan Valley.[1]

Pelota and *pala* became major pastimes for Basque men enjoying their vacations. It was another opportunity to relax and to enjoy the games they had played as boys in the Old Country. "I loved to play *pala*," recalled one Basque whose family's boardinghouse was across the street from Anduiza's fronton. "I lived it. Every chance we got, we played. We even played with golf balls." The equipment was difficult to acquire, though Big Jack Anduiza often made the handballs himself. Basque handballs are almost as hard as baseballs, tight and with little bounce, and *pelota* requires regular training to build up calluses so that the pain of the contact will be bearable. Boarders, especially those who had not played *pelota* for months or years, had difficulty getting back into the sport, though they would never admit it to opponents, John Anduiza suggested. "They would hit that ball, and in maybe four or five points their hands would swell up." The players would then seek out Big Jack. "He'd use this wooden board to step on their hands to take the swelling out [Big Jack weighed 240 pounds]. They'd go back and play five more points. Those guys from the Old Country were tough."[2]

The games were usually for pleasure, though shortly after the construction of the frontons, competitions between teams, often from two different towns, were organized for more serious stakes—money. In September 1920 Mountain Home's Vergara "Motxa" Chacartegui and Pascual Chacartegui challenged Henry Alegria and Manual Yribar, both from Boise. More than fifty people traveled from Boise to Mountain Home to see the match, which took place at Pedro "Askartxa" Anchustegui's fronton and offered $150 to the winning team. The Mountain Home duo won 50-44. According to Henry Alegria, "The Mountain Home players did not beat us; it was Anchustegui with his bad balls." Before the match, each team got to select two balls for service, but "the game was delayed for a long time that Sunday afternoon arguing about the balls. [Pedro Anchustegui] would repair or sew their ball . . . but wouldn't repair ours. Towards the end of the game, my . . . partner Manuel got so mad he couldn't return half the balls." The Boise team got their revenge the following Wednesday at Anduiza's, winning 50-28. "We got our money back, and both days we played to capacity houses."[3]

The Basque sports, with their clacking and loud applause, began to draw an audience of townspeople. At the Star Rooming House curious firemen from the nearby Boise City Fire Department climbed the fronton wall to watch the games. The *Idaho Statesman* sent a reporter to cover the first match ever played at Anduiza's fronton, on January 29, 1915. Standing among the crowd gathered in the balcony and at court level, the reporter watched the Boise team beat visitors from Shoshone in a close match that ended 50-48. "Shouts and hurrahs coming from the vicinity of Sixth and Grove Streets caused some conjecture as to what might be the matter Friday afternoon," he wrote. "It is an odd game played in a walled court, the ball is batted about with small paddles." He praised "the prowess of the locals" and the participation of the "Spaniards," who were "deeply engaged. . . . This game means as much to the [Basques] as baseball and football do to the Americans."[4]

Basque celebrations, especially Christmas and New Year's parties, were also becoming noticeable to others. The boardinghouses were overflowing for the holidays ("I would have to share my room," the son of one owner recalled), and the women would prepare the best meals of the year. In Boise one boardinghouse worker said, "Every New Year's Eve, at midnight, each boardinghouse group, with their musicians and men and women, would go out on Main Street and congregate at the Eastman Building (on Eighth and Main Streets). The American people would come out from their homes just to watch us." She said they would dance in the intersection for a while, then skip in a snake line through downtown restaurants and hotel lobbies. The local paper recorded later: "New Year's Eve was a blaze of color. . . . [Basques] marched and sang, a gay, merry, brilliant group."[5]

Cultures Clash

Idahoans' exposure to Basques in the early decades of the twentieth century was fleeting; they were a curiosity concealed behind boardinghouse doors, stoic faces that could not communicate. The boardinghouses, which were so effective in helping Basques take their first wobbly steps into mainstream America, also kept them from completely assimilating with Idahoans and added to the Basques' clannish image. They served as small fortresses for the immigrants, places where they could retreat and not have to speak English or associate with Anglo-Americans. Without these early enclaves, Basque communities in Idaho might have dissipated before they were even noticed.[6]

As it was, the small clusters of Basques in towns throughout the southern part of the state kept to themselves, ventured out only when necessary, and learned little English. Basque women pointed and pantomimed their way through Idaho's shops and associated almost exclusively with other Basques. The men usually worked alone in the sheep industry, where their rare lessons in English were obscene chastisements from cowboys or unintelligible sessions with camptenders or passersby. Even if they did work with others, they likely joined fellow Basques on construction crews or ranches, where their English would certainly not improve. Most of them simply lacked opportunities or reasons to learn English, and the efforts of those who tried often resulted in embarrassment. One brave herder frequented a restaurant in Mountain Home and hoped to acquire some English by speaking with the waiters. He became frustrated after several weeks and told a Basque friend he would never learn English. His friend told him that he was right; he definitely would not learn, at least not at that particular restaurant—the Chinese family who ran it couldn't speak English either.[7]

Lacking a command of the English language was not the only impediment to assimilation. Cultural traits passed down for generations in the Basque Country had been brought to Idaho, and some included social habits that did not always blend. One of the most obvious differences was the Basque proclivity for celebrations, especially celebrations with wine and spirits during much-anticipated breaks from long stretches of labor. In places like the Merino Bar in Boise or the Spanish Pool Hall in Shoshone, Basques enjoyed themselves by relaxing and visiting with friends. To people unfamiliar with the hard work that Basque men did on ranches and in mills, or unfamiliar with their bar rituals, they might have appeared to be pool hall loiterers and gamblers. In the Basque Country it was common to stroll from bar to bar, stopping briefly for a drink. "They were doing that here, too," said one Basque woman, "going from boardinghouse to boardinghouse." They were conspicuous in the streets, traveling in packs, noticeable for their work clothes, sharp features, and dark hair.[8]

Most of the men, as one former herder described it, had for months been "living like animals. . . . You had to come to town and be humanized again, so you spent everything, you got drunk, and you danced with the girls. You became another person." The restrictions of their hometowns were thousands of miles away, and they were usually carrying wads of cash from the annual wage payments. Although most of the Basques were conscious of saving money, occasionally their behavior was less than puritan. One elderly Basque said, "There might be forty to fifty boys in the house in the wintertime, and some of them would get drunk as hell and go to some of the whores." They might visit a brothel or seek out "chippies," streetwalkers. Some of them acquired venereal diseases, which, in the days before fast treatment was available, could put them out of work for months.[9]

Some of the men would blow their salaries during the holidays. "We had several clubs in town that would get these guys and oil 'em up," one owner recalled. "And when you get oiled up, you'd do anything, spend two or three hundred dollars in one night." Others would get into poker games or bet on handball matches and lose a good portion of the money they should have been sending home.[10]

Their social acceptance of alcohol clashed with a progressive anti-saloon movement that began in Idaho shortly after the turn of the century. The temperance movement grew, and in 1916 Idaho governor Moses Alexander approved legislation prohibiting alcohol throughout the state; local communities worked vigorously to enforce it. In December 1915 a Basque herder wrote home: "I have been able to save some money, and after the first of the year I will save even more because they have taken away all drinking in the state." He added, "[This Christmas] I'm going to town for only fifteen to twenty days, because on New Year's Day, they're taking away all the drinks except lemonade and cider. We have to drink everything we can now. . . . This [Prohibition] came about because the women in this country can vote, and they rule just as men do in Spain."[11]

Local governments moved swiftly to enforce Prohibition. In Boise, Mayor Jeremiah Robinson arranged for police raids of designated establishments. Boardinghouses scrambled to finish or hide all their wine and liquor. Lucy Garatea said the Star Rooming House had a special place "under the steps" to stash its alcohol. Another Basque woman remembered that the boardinghouse she lived next to in Mountain Home kept a cleverly hidden still in the back lot, and they kept their liquor in a box under her parents' outhouse.[12]

For people who had worked hard for months and were ready to cut loose, Prohibition was difficult to accept—and the boardinghouses commiserated with them. They often accepted the consequences of a police raid in order to continue serving wine and *café royals*. Moreover, competition had arisen between the boardinghouses in some Basque communities, and if one had an accordion for dancing on Sundays, the other had to have a piano; if one served steak, the others had to as well. If one was serving jiggers of whiskey in its dining room, then the others would have to—or lose business. During Prohibition "all the boardinghouses had liquor," one owner claimed. The son of one proprietor remembered that at his parents' boardinghouse, three blocks from the state capitol, "we always kept a bottle or two hidden. It was moonshine, paid five dollars a gallon for it. We were raided but never caught like some of the other places. In fact, that's how we paid the doctor, with a shot of whiskey!"[13]

The liquor was often smuggled in from Canada, sometimes Montana. One Boisean driving through Montana with his Basque grandfather in the 1980s was amazed at how many back roads and shortcuts the older man knew. His grandfather explained, "This is exactly where we used to bring our moonshine through." Others resorted to producing their own liquor in stills or concocting recipes for home brew. Once acquired, booze was distributed to any boardinghouse that needed it, then sold for twenty-five cents a jigger at parties and dances, where the doors were locked and guarded in case of police raids. Unwanted police visits constantly threatened boardinghouses, but owners' lack of legal discretion was replaced by a knack for creative hiding places. One woman remembered that during a police raid on her parents' boardinghouse, she was given a bottle of whiskey and told to put it inside the toilet and then to sit on the seat. When the police opened the door to the bathroom, they said, "Oh, excuse me," and went on. Other women hid their bottles under their shirts and pretended to be nursing a baby.[14]

The tricks did not always work. "The policemen knew what was going on," one woman said. It was a gamble. A boardinghouse could distribute liquor and make a bundle or it could get caught and have to face the penalties. One former boardinghouse maid recalled that her employer, after working feverishly to smuggle a case of whiskey from Canada, sold a bottle of it to a stranger who happened to be an undercover policeman. Court records after 1916 are peppered with the names of

Basques charged for possession of liquor. In 1917 one Basque man was caught outside Mountain Home with ninety-six quarts of whiskey in his truck; another was accused of transporting nine barrels of whiskey in his wagon. In a 1917 criminal case against a Basque man, the State of Idaho exhibited a two-quart bottle of wine, twenty-seven quarts of Sunnybrook Whiskey, one ten-gallon keg of whiskey ("about $^1/_3$ full"), one glass jug of whiskey, and one stone jug of whiskey. Mysteriously, the case was dismissed due to insufficient evidence.[15]

Basques' views of liquor offered one of the strongest clashes of culture in Idaho, but aside from the infractions during Prohibition (and the grazing disputes), they were rarely involved in any other illegal activity. An incident in March 1911 was one of the few exceptions. Two Basque boardinghouses in Boise were raided by police officers, who later charged them with running improper rooming houses. The owners were fined a total of six hundred dollars. At one of the boardinghouses, located at Ninth and Front Streets, the police arrested two Anglo-American women and charged them with vagrancy. The officers claimed the hotel owners had "created a bawdy house." Later, the *Idaho Daily Statesman* reported that the four "Spaniards who own the hotel . . . attempted to prove that they were not aware of conditions which prevailed at the hotel, and stated that they were trying to improve the character of the place." They were found guilty and fined one hundred dollars apiece. The next day, the headline smirked: ROOMING HOUSE PROPRIETORS ENRICH COFFERS OF CITY.[16]

Yet this was a period of exceptions. In general, Basque immigrant morality fit in well in their new home. Herders were well policed in the boardinghouse environment. One herder remembered that if he "went overboard," the owner would "chew me out: 'Zu atzo moskorra zinan!' [You were drunk yesterday!] There was no monkey business. You needed that." The maids and boardinghouse families would also help control things. One owner said, "We'd look out for them, especially the younger ones that came from the Old Country: 'Don't do this,' and, 'Don't go over there.' 'Take care of your money and go to the bank.'" They sometimes offered rewards. One boardinghouse owner is reported to have given free shots of whiskey on Sundays to the boarders who had gone to mass. At other times they left consequences. One of the few medical services the Socorros Mutuos did not cover was treatment for venereal disease.[17]

Religious Tradition with a Twist

Infrequent incidents aside, Basques were generally regarded by their new neighbors as law-abiding, moral, and honest. Many attributed this to their strong religious beliefs. Although they had moved into an over-whelmingly Protestant state, Basques were respected for their strong Catholic tradition. Even though they were slower to convert than other groups in the Iberian Peninsula, Basques had become "the most ardent Catholics in Spain." Their Catholicism "is simple, natural and unques-tioning, lacking in any display of emotion or sentiment," wrote one folklorist. Their agrarian past, one priest commented, "allowed them to understand the flow of life, a kind of primitive spirituality." They main-tained a distant respect for the clergy, though for some it was accom-panied by resentment. One Basque woman recalled, "When we were young, my family was very poor, but the priests lived well. We even had to give from what little we had to the priest. That didn't seem right to me." Others recalled the reply Basques offered when asked by friends how they were doing: "Abadiak obeto" (The priests are doing better).[18]

Basques immigrating to Idaho came from a tradition where Catholi-cism dominated most aspects of their lives, from their festivals to their clothes. "We had to go [to mass]," one man claimed. "We were under compulsion." While the women stood in the front of the church, he said, "the men would come late, stand in the back, and leave early."[19]

Basques who moved to Idaho followed this tradition in a somewhat different form. Many immigrants, perhaps harboring resentment for the clergy or enjoying freedom from their strict backgrounds, stopped going to church altogether. In one survey, 118 of 119 Basque immigrants said they were Catholic, but almost half the men polled did not attend church. Free from societal obligation, and employed in isolated areas, they did not make church a priority. "When you are herding sheep," a former herder suggested, "you don't have the chance to go, and after six years I lost the habit." One resident at several Basque hotels said, "I can't recall one young guy dressing up and going to church on a Sunday morning."[20]

Most Basques, however, clung to Catholicism as an important ele-ment of their lives. Many of the men, employed in town, and almost all the women continued to attend church after immigrating. One lo-cal priest described them as "deeply religious." In many areas of Idaho,

Basques represented a large portion of the Catholic population, and they even helped build the first Catholic churches in some towns. In Jordan Valley, just across the Oregon border, Basques collaborated with several Irish families in 1914 to construct a stone church, the first in town. Occasionally services were offered in Euskera.[21]

Basque attendance at mass was increasingly noticeable to Idaho Catholics in the first decade of the century. By 1910 Bishop Alphonse Glorieux of Boise wrote to the bishop in Araba, requesting a priest to serve the growing Basque community in southern Idaho. The Basque bishop responded by dispatching Father Bernardo Arregui, who in July 1911 was given pastoral responsibility for all the Basques in Idaho.[22]

While serving as an associate at St. John's Cathedral in Boise, Father Arregui administered the Catholic sacraments to Basques throughout southern Idaho. In 1918 it was suggested to the diocese that Father Arregui become pastor of a new church exclusively for Basques. The diocese accepted. Bishop Daniel M. Gorman approved the purchase of two buildings on the corner of Fifth and Idaho, one to be converted to a church, the other the pastor's residence. The location was perfect, only a few minutes' walk from most Boise boardinghouses.[23]

The Church of the Good Shepherd, the only Basque church in the United States, was blessed by Bishop Gorman on Sunday morning, March 2, 1919. Just in time for the occasion, a group of singers from St. John's Cathedral joined local Basques to form the Good Shepherd Choir, which at the blessing sang "Ecce Sacerdos Magnus" (Behold a Great Priest). Bishop Gorman and Father Arregui then celebrated the opening mass. After a brief sermon in English by Bishop Gorman, Father Arregui, delivering his homily in Euskera, reminded the packed congregation that they shared blood "that ran in the veins of St. Ignatius of Loyola" and encouraged them to "follow the path worthy of your blood and race, as you are doing at the present." He recognized the church as "an ornament to this hospitable city in which you live and to which you owe so much, and a joy and satisfaction to your parents who live on the other side of the broad Atlantic." He concluded that the church would be "an inestimable inheritance for your children."[24]

Services at the Church of the Good Shepherd were well attended by Basques, especially women, many of whom went to daily mass. "It was such a nice little church," recalled one former Basque neighbor. "It fit about one hundred people. I can remember people coming to Boise from miles away just to get married there." An anthropologist once described the three most important symbols for a Basque community as the church, representing faith; the cemetery, representing tradition; and a handball court, representing a vibrant outdoor life. With the Church of the Good Shepherd, Basques in Idaho had all three. Furthermore, it signaled the transformation of a significant portion of the Basque population from itinerant herders to settled city dwellers. Their lives changed, as did the impressions of the wider American audience.[25]

The Gates Close

Even though the Basques had their own church, hotels, insurance agencies, and place in the sheep industry, they were just a tiny pocket of ethnicity in the United States. Millions of other Europeans had made the same Atlantic crossing and had formed their own enclaves in East Coast cities and Midwest farm towns. Although America did not always look favorably on the masses pouring into the country, and despite recurrent movements to stop immigration, the government's hands-off immigration policy neither officially encouraged nor discouraged those who wanted to enter the country. Immigration was rarely easy, and almost every group suffered prejudice ranging from verbal abuse to bloody lynching. Still, if immigrant groups could endure and dedicate themselves to a life of labor, with time they could feel a part of the nation.[26] By the 1920s, however, the United States began to close the gates as the country responded to a growing fear of undesirable newcomers. A movement spread to exclude those immigrants "who bring least money to the country and who come most quickly upon public or private charity for support," an indirect reference to southern and eastern Europeans. Moreover, the theories of Charles Darwin and Herbert Spencer seemed to support the belief that mixing races and ethnic groups harmed the species. This, added to the xenophobia of World War I and the initial stages of the Red Scare, created an urgency to stem the tide of immigration. In 1921 the United States established its first immigration quota law. Only 3 percent of the number recorded for any nationality in the 1910 Census would be allowed to enter. The Spanish quota, which included Basques, was 912 immigrants per year. The Immigration Act of 1924 reduced the number of Spanish nationals allowed annually to just 131. The law ended Basques' large-scale entry into the American West—or at least their legal entry.[27]

The nativistic attitude was evident in Idaho through prejudice inflicted upon immigrant groups. After the completion of the transcontinental railway, many Chinese moved to Idaho and labored in the thriving mining industry. Idaho Territory recorded 4,274 Chinese in the 1870 Census. Then, partly because of racism and partly because American workers felt that their jobs were threatened, Congress passed the Chinese Exclusion Act of 1882, which prevented Chinese immigration for ten years. (The act was later renewed indefinitely.) Mid-1880s headlines in Idaho newspapers echoed the prejudice: THE CHINESE MUST GO, and HOW TO GET RID OF THE CHINESE. By 1900 Idaho's Chinese population had declined to 1,500, and by the 1920s only several hundred remained.[28]

In 1900 there were 6,000 Germans in Idaho, a large enough concentration to found the Turnverein Hall, a German cultural institution, in 1906. But World War I created a new antipathy toward Idaho's German community. In 1916 the Turnverein Hall was sold, and Germans in Idaho, like Germans throughout the country, suppressed expressions of their ethnic heritage. As Idaho historian Merle Wells wrote, "With a German population larger than any other group's at the time, Boise suffered a substantial cultural loss."[29]

The Basque experience in Idaho was very different. "One of the most significant features of the acculturation and assimilation process of the Basques in Idaho," one sociologist wrote, "has been the almost complete lack of prejudice and discrimination." In a survey of 119 Basque immigrants, not one reported any serious or organized intimidation. There had been isolated instances during the Spanish-American War, but not on the scale of those experienced by Germans during World War I. The Basques' physical and cultural differences were not great enough to inflame discriminatory attitudes, unlike the response to other ethnic groups such as the Chinese, and later the Japanese. Moreover, the prejudice that did exist all but dissipated when Basques made their homes in Idaho.[30]

Because Basques were willing to take the jobs nobody else wanted, they did not threaten the occupational status of established Idahoans. Furthermore, most possessed traits that blended well with American values. Many had an instinct for entrepreneurship that thrived in American capitalism, and after several years in the country, dozens created their own businesses. In 1916 José Anacabe started Anacabe Transfer in Boise, "one of the earliest long-distance hauling systems in Idaho." Joe and Benny Garate operated their own taxi service. John Archabal ran one of the largest sheep operations in the nation. By the 1920s he was one of the wealthiest men in Idaho.[31]

By this time, thousands of Basques had established a community in Idaho that satisfied their practical needs and, for most, made life much happier than it had been back home. Most had come to herd sheep and not only became competent but also thrived. Idaho sheepmen jumped at the chance to hire them. Basques rose to every level of the industry, from foreman to camptender to owner. Others had moved into entirely different occupations—carpentry, farming, and bartending.[32]

Although not all Basques experienced this level of success and some, indeed, returned home penniless, most surpassed any goals they had had when they first arrived. They survived their difficult years as "economic refugees" and acquired bank accounts and ways of life unattainable for their parents and neighbors in the Basque Country. They established a solid foundation for later immigrants and for their children. They had not completely blended into American society, but they made assimilation possible for their children. Idahoans started to recognize it. "Many [Basques] return to their native province after a few years here have awarded them substantial livelihoods," the local paper reported in the late 1920s. "But almost to a man they return only for a visit and after a few months they are back here again. [America] is the land of their adoption, and they make good citizens."[33]

Bermeo, Bizkaia, 1920s. Most Basque immigrants came from small Bizkaian villages of several hundred people—and most had never ventured far from these hometowns before undertaking the seven-thousand-mile trip to Idaho. Courtesy Basque Museum, Boise, Idaho.

For centuries, Basques have farmed on small family plots resting on steep inclines. The physical challenges they faced in the American West were not necessarily tougher than scratching out a living back home. Courtesy Basque Museum, Boise, Idaho.

A baserri *in Navarniz, Bizkaia. Most immigrants grew up in these typical farmhouses, stone structures warmed only by kitchen fireplaces and the body heat of animals residing in barn stalls on the ground floor. Courtesy Basque Museum, Boise, Idaho.*

Felipe Arriola and Agustina Garachana were married in 1915 in Ispaster, Bizkaia. However, most Basque men and women came alone and met their future spouses in Idaho. Courtesy Basque Museum, Boise, Idaho.

Basque herders on a break, ca. 1905. A Caldwell, Idaho, newspaper reported in 1909 that Basques were "filthy, treacherous and meddlesome" and unless measures were taken, they would "make life impossible for the white man." Courtesy Basque Museum, Boise, Idaho.

Boarders at Boise's Modern Hotel, ca. 1900. By the turn of the century, there were dozens of boardinghouses serving Basques throughout the state. For lonely immigrants, they were temporary homes, hospitals, the places they met and married their spouses. Courtesy Basque Museum, Boise, Idaho.

Basques gathering in Boise for a reception honoring two newly married immigrant couples, 1917. Such marriages often cemented decisions to stay permanently in the United States. Courtesy Basque Museum, Boise, Idaho.

Boarders and employees of Boise's Modern Hotel, 1925. Many Basque herders binged during rare visits to town, causing some Idahoans to view them as "pool hall loiterers and gamblers." Courtesy Basque Museum, Boise, Idaho.

Christmas dinner at a Boise boardinghouse, 1931. Like most businesspeople, boardinghouse owners suffered during the Depression but were happy once again to serve alcohol legally when Prohibition was behind them. Courtesy Basque Museum, Boise, Idaho.

Jose Navarro's sheep camp in Jordan Valley, Oregon, near the Idaho border, ca. 1915. From the earliest days, Basques helped make the state's sheep industry— though most of them could hardly wait to move on to other occupations. Courtesy Basque Museum, Boise, Idaho.

Many Basques agreed that the physical rigors of herding were nothing compared to the mental challenges. Herders would go weeks or months without seeing another human during the summer grazing season. Courtesy Basque Museum, Boise, Idaho.

John Archabal (formerly Juan Achabal) in front of a sheep wagon at a Sheepherders' Ball, 1930s. Archabal immigrated to Idaho penniless in 1893 but became one of the wealthiest men in the state. He started the Sheep-herders' Ball in 1929 as an annual charity fund-raiser, and at the end of the century the dances were still among the most anticipated events of the year in Basque communities throughout the state. Courtesy Basque Museum, Boise, Idaho.

In 1911 Father Bernardo Arregui was sent from the Basque Country to serve the Basque community in southern Idaho. He eventually became pastor of the Church of the Good Shepherd in Boise—the only Basque church in the United States. Courtesy Basque Museum, Boise, Idaho.

The Church of the Good Shepherd, completed in 1919. Father Arregui called the church "an ornament to this hospitable city." Just two years later, however, Idaho's bishop closed it to Basques' exclusive use, and it became his private chapel. Courtesy Basque Museum, Boise, Idaho.

Three women display the flag of the American Basque Fraternity, 1933. These social organizations assisted Basques with their needs and helped them blend into their new country. One group's by-laws promised to "foster and promote Americanization of its members." Courtesy Basque Museum, Boise, Idaho.

Savino Uberuaga, dubbed the "Bounding Basque" by local reporters, was the son of Basque immigrants who became an outstanding football player for Boise High School in the mid-1930s. Sports were a strong means of assimilation for second-generation Basques, many of whom excelled in high school athletics throughout the state. Courtesy Basque Museum, Boise, Idaho.

II

The Hyphenated Generation

The Bilbao family began to grow. Frank and Frances had three children—Dolores, Julio, and Frankie. Though both of the parents spoke Basque, none of the children were raised speaking it. In fact, Frank seemed to be purposely raising the children in a way that would ease their adjustment to American life. "Mom and Dad only spoke Basque when they didn't want us to know the full scoop," one of their children later said.

The children attended public schools in Cascade, encouraged by their parents to take full advantage. "There was one thing we understood from the beginning," Julio said. "The message was that education is the most important thing in the world, and if you're going to have opportunities, you've got to have an education. So it was just expected that we were going to go on to school."

All three of Frank and Frances Bilbao's children were influenced by their relations with the Basque boarders at the Emery Hotel, Julio said. "Any work that was done around the hotel by Basques was competition. You could go out and get a load of wood, you could go cut trees, you could shovel snow, you could help them mix cement. When you watch Basques work, it's competition: 'Let's see if anyone can keep up with us.' I saw that at a very early age. It wasn't enough just to bring in an armful of wood. It was, 'Let's see how high I can pile this wood.' That's the way they operate—in everything. I don't know if that transferred into my competitiveness or Frankie's competitiveness, but we were very successful in athletics. We both excelled in everything: football, basketball, track and field."

Julio graduated from Carroll College in Helena, Montana, in 1966. That summer, he and Frankie took a trip to Europe. They traveled to England, Denmark, Germany, Austria, and eventually to France on their way to the Basque Country to see their father's family. "We came on a train across southern France," Julio said. "I will never forget as we got to the [Franco-Spanish] border, and seeing all these Basque names at the train stations and recognizing them. And then hearing the Basque spoken. I remember going to Bermeo [in Bizkaia], and it was so beautiful for me. There was some kind of feeling that went right down to your bones: 'This is it. This is where *amuma* [grandma] is from. This is where our people have been forever.' And it was a tingling experience to sense that. To go to the *baserris* [sic] and see our families. It was just so much more colorful and meaningful than I thought it would be. We met my dad's mother, Francesca Ausocoa, on that visit. She was ninety years old and had witnessed the bombing of Guernica [Gernika] in 1936.

"That first trip piqued my interest and sense of pride. We were treated so well by the family that I had a new sense of the word 'family,' because I had never felt that way before." The 1966 trip, Julio said, "really gave me the *gogoa* [drive]" to want to explore and advance the knowledge of Basque culture upon his return to Idaho.

+= =+

After his first trip to the Basque Country, Julio Bilbao went to graduate school at Idaho State University in Pocatello. He met a young woman there named Julie Egurrola, a nursing student from Homedale, Idaho, who had also grown up in a Basque home. Julio recalled that he was attracted by their common background. "In the back of my mind," Julio said, "it was a Basque person I was looking for [to marry]. I felt like somebody with a Basque background would probably understand who I was better than somebody else would."

Their backgrounds really were quite similar: They both had been raised by Basque parents in small Idaho towns. They had been taught English from birth, but their parents' Basque influence was indelible. Julie remembered being surprised by this when they first met at Idaho State University. "I knew Julio was Basque, but for me it was no big deal. People are people." But for Julio, she said, the 1966 trip to the Basque Country had been a moving experience. "It was like a transformation for him. Because it was so important for him, it became more important for me. He made the Basque thing more real, and something that you worked at. It didn't just happen to you. You worked at it."

+= =+

Julio and Julie were married in 1968, and they moved to Boise, where Julio took a job at South Junior High School teaching history.

After three years Julio decided to take a leave of absence to study in the history department of the University of Nevada, Reno, which under Dr. William A. Douglass offered a Ph.D. in Basque studies. Though he decided not to pursue the full degree, his time in Reno compelled him to want to study Basque culture in more depth. After returning to Boise, Julio volunteered for the Idaho Basque Studies Committee, which had been created by a grant from the National Endowment for the Humanities.

One of the program's first major projects was the 1972 Basque Holiday Festival, which Julio and Julie volunteered to help organize. Julie remembered, "I made little costumes for the girls for the costume contest, these little jota outfits. I didn't know what I was going to do for the little white scarves that are supposed to go with the costume. Well, I had to go buy white pants for Julio, and of course, you always have to cut the legs off the bottom because they are so long. I cut about [five inches] off and the girls' heads fit right into those pant legs. That was the girls' kerchief."

⊨ ⊨

I n the summer of 1972, Julio Bilbao was part of the group that traveled to the Basque Country for six weeks of study sponsored by the Idaho Basque Studies Program. It had a different impact on him than the first trip had. "I came back more politically aware about what was going on over there." He was also aware of the threat that Franco's dictatorship was posing to the Basque language. It was important to him that his daughters meet Jon Oñatibia, the musician and teacher that the Basque Studies Program brought to Boise to teach Basque music, dancing, and language. "I wanted the kids to know Oñatibia and be around him, because I knew that there was more to Basque than just the strange tongue. I wanted my girls to understand the pride of the Basques. No question about it. I knew the girls weren't going to learn to speak Basque in playing Jon's little songs, but I thought they'd at least have an affinity for Basque culture. Then maybe their curiosity and sense of pride [would] cause them to do more. And that's exactly what happened." Julio Bilbao's involvement with the Idaho Basque Studies Program was also a success, he thought. "I'm really proud of what that small group was able to do from 1971 to 1974. The program resuscitated the interest in the language. It was just accepted before that Basque was kind of dead, and kids couldn't learn Basque, so why bother teaching it?"

5

Into the Crucible

W hen the Basque emigrates," Rodney Gallop observed in 1930, "he becomes a different man. He throws off his clogging conservatism . . . and develops unsuspected qualities of energy and initiative. But there is a risk that he may cease, to all intents and purposes, to be a Basque."[1] Basques in Idaho had joined the dozens of other immigrant groups around the United States who were conforming to established American principles at an unprecedented pace. "Here you stand in your fifty groups, with your fifty languages and histories, and your fifty blood hatreds and rivalries," one author observed after visiting Ellis Island. "Germans and Frenchmen, Irishmen and Englishmen, Jews and Russians—into the crucible with you all! God is making the American."[2]

Children of Basque immigrants attended American schools, ate American food, danced American dances, played American sports, sang American songs, and dated other Americans. They were raised in Basque culture at home, yet the momentum of Americanizing influences and the historical circumstances in which they grew up moved them into mainstream life. As does each generation, they faced their choices and opportunities. Clearly they saw their future in America, yet some felt that it was important to hold on to elements of the past culture.

Although the second generation especially moved into conventional Anglo-American life, the American initiation began when their parents entered the United States. Perhaps the most dramatic alteration took place with one of their most basic possessions—their names. Some Basques had their names involuntarily modified at their point of entry; others changed them to sound more American. "Enrique" Alegria wrote that soon after his family moved to Idaho from Bizkaia, "We began calling ourselves American names. Ignacio became Ignace, I became Henry." Basques with the surname Uriaguerica became Uria, Malaxechevarria became Berria, Cenarusabeitia became Beitia, and, to the relief of many tongues, Estaquio Garroguerricaechevarria became Ed Garro. One Basque sheepherder in the Sun Valley area even took the name of his employer's ranch. Many Basque women, accustomed to keeping their maiden name after marriage in the Old Country, also began to conform to the American system of taking the husband's surname.[3]

The cultural organizations that Basques formed highlight the trend. Although these associations sponsored many Basque activities, their by-laws reflected an American emphasis. La Fraternidad Vasca Americana (American Basque Fraternity), founded in 1928 to "render financial aid and assistance to its members when in distress," was patterned after the Eagles, a local American fraternal organization. The organization, intended to help immigrant Basques adapt to their new country, existed also "to encourage, foster and promote Americanization of its members, by aiding and assisting those who are not naturalized citizens of the United States to familiarize themselves with its constitution and laws and become citizens thereof." Another objective was "to provide facilities for and encourage the learning and use of the English language." This group pledged to "encourage, foster, conduct and hold games of handball, baseball, football, golf, lawn tennis, and all classes of athletic amusements and sports."[4]

While Basques may have had to change their names or form specific organizations to fit into society, their drive to get ahead matched well with the American work ethic. Typical of immigrants, Basques looked to advance when the opportunity arose. Of 119 Basque immigrants interviewed in the 1940s, 75 percent had first worked as sheepherders in Idaho. But one-third had left the industry after two years, and by the mid-1940s only 26 percent remained in the sheep business. Some had learned enough English to take jobs requiring interaction with Idahoans. In the 1920s, for example, many Basque men took jobs several miles east of Boise with the Boise-Payette Lumber Company (later,

Boise-Cascade Corporation) at a mill in Barber, the company town that was eventually swallowed up by Boise. Later, when the mill was moved to Emmett, most of the Basque families moved with it.[5]

Basques continued to establish their own businesses. In Nampa, Candido Mendiguren bought a shoe-repair business in 1912 that he operated until 1959. In Boise, "Pete" Mendieta, who had been a barber in the Spanish military, opened the O.K. Barber Shop. Known as Barbero, he was the first in the state to register for a barber's license when the legislature required it. Barbero was a fixture in downtown Boise, cutting hair for thirty-three years in his shop in the Egyptian Theater building.[6]

The Basque immigrants' success also allowed them to take their biggest step into American culture, the purchase of their first homes. "The Basque colony here has prospered," an Idaho newspaper reported in 1931. "The visitor who goes through Boise streets and notices the many substantial dwellings in Spanish style which adorn the various thoroughfares can bear witness to that." Besides a financial and physical commitment to American life, buying homes meant they would also have more interaction with American neighbors.[7]

Still, the changes that immigrants made were mostly material and superficial. Inside their homes, they still ate Basque food and spoke the Basque language. They socialized almost exclusively with Basque friends, playing cards, visiting in pool halls, and celebrating family occasions. For their children, this meant an almost exclusively Basque upbringing during their preschool years. Although many immigrants had learned passable English by the time they had children, for most, the Basque lifestyle was still the path of least resistance: according to one study, Euskera was spoken in almost 90 percent of the immigrants' homes. While the parents had enjoyed opportunities in America that they never would have had in the Basque Country, they were still immigrants who had spent their formative years in another language and culture. One Basque woman remembered her immigrant mother continually saying, "Oh, the opportunity in this country. If I would have been born and gone to school in this country, I could have really done something."[8]

Although they themselves did not have the opportunity, the immigrant generation wanted their children to enjoy the advantages that a good education and the ability to speak English would bring. For the Basque children, as for other American-born children of immigrants, the school system was perhaps the single most Americanizing force. In many ways, the children's first walks to school represented the Basques' first real steps into American society.

Rough Days at School

If American-born Basque children learned any English by their first day at school, it was probably spoken with a Basque accent, telltale rolled r's and thick vowels. One Basque wrote to Bizkaia in 1927 with the news that his two-year-old daughter "speaks half Basque and half American." The second generation of Basques might have picked up a smattering of English words playing with non-Basque children in their neighborhoods. "Around the boarding houses," the *Idaho Statesman* reported in 1941, "ran broods of handsome, sooty-eyed children; and with them ran an assortment of blue and gray eyed offspring of Idaho pioneers." One man remembered that even in his predominantly Basque neighborhood on Grove Street in Boise, he played American games with other children: "Shinny [street hockey], kick the can, run sheep run, and baseball." Other children might have learned to mimic English words that they heard on the earliest radio programs.[9]

Yet most Basque children, particularly the family's firstborn, went to school unable to speak any English. For the rest of their lives, many would vividly recall their first days of class, the experience of hearing the teacher blathering in words they could not recognize. "When I went to school," one woman recalled, "I couldn't talk American. And I had to go to the bathroom so bad! But I didn't know how to say it. So I peed all over the floor."[10]

Sometimes the children were fortunate enough to live in areas heavily populated with Basques, and when they gathered at recess to play, they could speak the language they had grown up with. Basque names were sprinkled throughout class rolls in southern Idaho and eastern Oregon: "Ignacio Anduiza . . . Pilar Argoitia . . . Janice Davis . . . Jimmy Donovan . . . Peter Johnson . . . Louis Odiaga." One Jordan Valley elementary school teacher remembered that in 1926, twenty-two of her twenty-seven students were American-born Basques. But even then, teachers would often forbid the children to speak Euskera in class and on the playground. One second-generation woman said dozens of children in her Mountain Home elementary school were Basques. "All those kids couldn't speak English," she said. "We would get to school and we'd speak in Basque, and the teacher would say [rapping on the desk], 'We don't speak Basque in this room! We speak English!'"[11]

Their inability to speak English made them targets of other children's cruelty. Children would hear their Basque classmates speaking a strangely coded language among themselves or their mumbled, accented attempts at English. Later they were branded as "black Bascos" or "garlic snappers," words used earlier by cowboys arguing with sheepherders over grazing land. They got into more than a few fistfights on the playgrounds. One elderly American-born Basque claimed, "If they called us 'black Basco,' we'd just knock the holy hell out of them until they stopped." Another second-generation Basque recalled that he carried rocks in his pocket on the way to and from school in case he was accosted by a group of bullies.[12]

The taunting they received at school, combined with the forces of the Americanizing environment, dissuaded children from speaking Basque and propelled them toward English. In elementary school the Basque language made them foreign and unusual at a time when they wanted to blend in and meet new playmates. "I started going to school, and I couldn't speak very good English," one second-generation Basque said. "I'd come home . . . and I was getting confused between the two languages. So the decision was made to just stick with the English." Another woman recalled a Basque family friend ridiculing her muddled attempts to speak Euskera as a child. "He kind of laughed at me and thought that my Basque was a little odd. He made some comment to my grandma and that embarrassed me, and from then on I started speaking English. I never spoke [Basque] again."[13]

Children learned English quickly and began using it with their siblings. "As I acquired English," a second-generation Basque said, "I became very proud of the new language and wanted to talk it all the time." This started a pattern whereby, from the oldest child to the youngest, knowledge of Euskera decreased, and the youngest children in Basque families would often be able to speak as much English as their non-Basque classmates on the first day of school. The local paper wrote: "One who started from Father Arregui's christening font as 'Pedro Esteban Antonio Ytuarte', with who knows how many lesser names, becomes upon entering the first grade of an American public school, merely—'Hey Pete!'"[14]

They were exposed to American history, government, music, sports, games, radio programs, comic books, and toys. "I think in English and translate to Basque when I talk that language," one second-generation Jordan Valley Basque said. "You see, my education is in English. In other words, I learned to describe my thoughts and feelings at school and, therefore, I learned your American way of thinking."[15]

After passing through the first grade, many second-generation Basques learned more English and American ways of behavior than most of their parents had learned after years in Idaho. All of them would have more formal education than their parents. In one study, the average schooling for foreign-born Basques was four years, while 12 percent had no formal schooling at all. By 1940, when only 30 percent of Idaho's population had a high school education, 73.7 percent of the second-generation Basques finished high school and 40 percent attended some college. This pattern initiated a role reversal in Basque families; the children's knowledge of English and their better education allowed them to help parents read forms, do their banking, go to the doctor—and it temporarily turned the Old World hierarchy of authority upside down.[16]

Whatever prejudice lingered from their early, awkward days at school disappeared, especially as young Basques began to excel at American sports. Basic athletic skills, combined with the work ethic acquired from their parents, allowed them to be successful in football, tennis, basketball, and baseball. In 1929 Boise Basques formed an American Legion baseball team. "We didn't have a coach," one of the players recalled, "just a bunch of us [Basque] guys playing ball." Still, they managed to finish second in their division. One of the early football stars at Boise High was Savino Uberuaga, who was nicknamed the Bounding Basque. On November 25, 1937, a local newspaper wrote, "The main worry of the Nampa Bulldogs in today's traditional holiday clash at Public School Field with the Boise Braves will be Savino Uberuaga who has proved the bolt in the Braves' lightning attack thus far this season." The newspaper praised the Bounding Basque, "he of the slippery hips on whom Boise will depend largely for a victory."[17]

The second generation was fulfilling many of the dreams of its immigrant parents. Supportive homes and good habits allowed these children to attend school and take advantage of its opportunities. The cultural differences they had manifested as nervous first-graders were disappearing, and they were taking their acquired Americanisms home with them. "The widow Garmendia still speaks the old tongue," the *Lewiston Morning Tribune* reported, "but her children answer her in English."[18]

6

The Decline of Basque Entry and Culture

The Americanization period for Basques coincided with a gradual closing of the gates for all immigration. Wives and children of Basques who had succeeded were still able to move to the western United States. Others might be chosen in the annual quota for Spanish nationals, though that possibility remained remote. For most young men in the Basque Country who wanted to emigrate to the United States after 1924, however, there was only one option: to enter the country illegally.

Gloves and doughnuts may be responsible for at least one Basque immigrant's illegal entry. Nick Beristain, employed on a ship carrying steel ingots from Bilbao to the eastern United States, saw stevedores working on a dock in New York. "A man would come and pass around gloves like they were biscuits in the morning. At ten-thirty, everybody stopped and they had coffee and doughnuts." He had never seen anything like this in the Basque Country, where dockworkers labored for subsistence wages. He thought to himself, "Hau da paisetxo, hau! [Now *this* is a country!]." He remembered, "That night another guy and I jumped ship."[1]

Even if such immigrants managed to sneak in successfully and make it across the country to Idaho, they still faced the challenge of finding employment, especially since they were illegal and at the mercy of their employers. Beristain said his boss cheated him out of about $500 after one of his first years of herding. Expecting to receive $225 a month as his annual payment, he received instead an unpleasant surprise. His employer told him, "I pay legal guys $225, but for you guys that are not legal, $175 . . . Hey, you don't got your papers, if you don't like it . . ." Later Beristain remembered, "So he paid me $175 a month for the year of work. As if my sheep knew I didn't have papers."[2]

Although Basques had been dropping out of the sheep industry as they found other work, herding was still the best available job for new Basque immigrants. In the 1920s there were as yet dozens of owners who were running sheep on trails throughout southern Idaho and eastern Oregon. In the Mountain Home area alone there were several small Basque companies averaging three to five bands, each with 2,200 to 3,000 head of sheep: Domingo Monasterio, Boni Oyarzabal, Domingo Aldecoa, Domingo Aguirre, and George Anchustegui, among others.[3]

These Basque owners helped newcomers out as much as possible, though the work was not much easier than for those who had preceded them. Lambing season in January and February remained the crucial time, as they had to watch day and night for ewes that might be having trouble delivering. The bloody process of castrating lambs demanded a hardy constitution. The herders cut the tip of the lamb's scrotum and pulled out the testicles with their teeth, spitting them into a bucket. Later, the testicles would be cleaned, cut, and cooked, a dish that became popularly known as Rocky Mountain oysters.[4]

In the long working days of March, the month for shearing, men clipped wool and stuffed it tightly into large sacks weighing nearly four hundred pounds. The sacks were loaded by handcart onto boxcars and shipped east for the next process. By the 1930s, Mountain Home was one of the largest wool-shipping points in the country; in 1934–35, 4.5 million pounds of wool were transported from the area. However, the boom faded as the full effects of the Depression permeated all sectors of the American economy. Even the sheep industry was not immune from its effects.[5]

The 1930s Depression and the Taylor Grazing Act

The stock market crash of 1929 and the Depression years that followed sent the United States economy into a downward spiral. The number of sheep in Idaho remained steady throughout these years, but the sad state of the economy as a whole rippled through the sheep industry, causing wool and lamb prices to plummet. Dan Archabal remembers lying in bed and hearing the footsteps of his father, John Archabal, as he paced the floor above him, worrying about securing adequate financing for the business.[6]

Basque women even formed another aid organization to help during these difficult times. La Organisación Independiente Sociale was founded in 1933, because, as one of its members explained, "so many people needed help." Established to contribute to its members' "instruction, assistance, recreation, clothing, medicine, or whatever may be needed," the association drew hundreds of women. The organization also offered some insurance and funeral benefits. When a member died, the organization's secretary collected one dollar from each member, added one hundred dollars from the general fund, and then presented the money to the family.[7]

The Depression was not the only event that affected the sheep industry during the 1930s. During this decade, the United States government got more involved in the eonomic life of the country than at any other time in history. This involvement extended to the sheep industry. Grazing fees and regulations had earlier been established by the U.S. Forest Service, but 170 million acres of land still remained in "the public domain," and the future of those acres was bitterly contested. Specifically, land legislation passed in the 1930s had ramifications for the sheep industry that severely changed the sheep business in the West. It ended the way of the itinerant herder and meant a larger commitment on the part of sheep owners.[8]

Pressure to regulate the large areas of public domain in the western United States had been growing for some time. The conservation movement, which resulted in the formation of the national park system under President Theodore Roosevelt, did not look favorably upon stories of the rapidly deteriorating open range of the West. Also, the image persisted that herders were raping the land and taking their money back to the Old Country. In the East a publicity campaign successfully portrayed this degeneration and blamed antiquated grazing practices as the culprit. Such sentiments, combined with demands from the livestock industry for additional grazing allotments on public lands, resulted in the passage of the Taylor Grazing Act of 1934.[9]

The bill and subsequent legislation allowed the Division of Grazing (later known as the Bureau of Land Management) to place 173 million acres in federal grazing districts. The act required fee payments and adherence to grazing schedules from those using the land. Moreover, all those who wanted to graze their animals on public land had to establish base property in order to be eligible. The Taylor Grazing Act closed ten western states, including Idaho, to itinerant herding. Allotments were to be determined by government officials and advisory boards comprised of locally settled ranchers, who denied access to sheepmen who did not own or lease private land. Basque sheepmen could no longer run their sheep freely on public lands. They were forced to make a much larger commitment if they wanted to stay in business. No other piece of legislation affected Basques like this one did. "Basques tend to reckon time in terms of before and after 'Taylor Grazing,'" wrote anthropologist William A. Douglass. He described "a kind of New and Old Testament in their group life in the American West."[10]

The Erosion of Immigrant Culture

The financial difficulties brought on by the Depression and the Taylor Grazing Act spelled the end for some Basques already here and for those yet to come. Within the Basque-American community, however, another set of forces was at work. "America's famed 'boiling pot' is working as fast in Idaho as it is in the metropolis of the east," Jack Beardwood, a journalist for the *Idaho Statesman,* noted in 1937. His observation appeared in an eight-part series on Basque history, religion, food, celebrations, and language. Although the articles had their share of inaccurate melodrama ("Into the Rocky Mountain region [Basques] flowed, their dark eyes searching for country suitable for the sheep herding they knew and loved so well"), they did manage to highlight the blending of Basques, especially those of the second generation, into American society.[11]

Because Basque immigrants spoke little English and stayed primarily within their ethnic enclave, they were viewed as clannish and reserved. Beardwood wrote: "In direct contrast to their parents the second generation Basques are not retiring and shy. They often are leaders in school affairs—athletics, dramatics, public speaking, scholarship." He added that second-generation Basques were employed in a wide spectrum of jobs, "jerking sodas, working in banks, driving trucks, tending filling stations, working in stores, performing secretarial duties." Tony Yturri, he wrote, was typical of the second generation: "He dresses well, is perfectly at home with Basques or Americans, has a good education, is drifting away from the Basque influence. . . . Yturri likes American dances, likes to date American girls. He's typically an American young man."[12]

It was inevitable, Beardwood said, that Basque culture in Idaho would be "covered with dust, obsolete, and . . . unremembered." He asserted that this was the common fate of immigrants. "They cannot withstand the influence of Americanism. Their customs are eroded as relentlessly as water erodes soil. The only method of combating it is to go into isolation." But Basques, he added, "are in daily contact with American forces. Because of this fact, their race will pass into oblivion as a distinct people."[13]

Things were changing. The first generation, in at least superficial aspects, adopted some characteristics that conformed to the American ideal. Despite the effects of the Depression and their flight from the declining sheep industry, almost 60 percent of first-generation Basques owned their own homes before World War II. Their frugality allowed them to survive the roughest economic times, and they were rarely forced to borrow. From 1922 to 1947 only two Basque families sought assistance from the Boise City Welfare Department, and only ten Basques were included on Idaho's old-age assistance rolls.[14]

Basque immigrants formed other organizations that clearly reflected a desire to fit into U.S. society. In April 1940 the Independent Order of Spanish-Basque Speaking People of Idaho filed for incorporation with the state. Formed by boardinghouse owners and leading sheepmen, the organization included representatives from Mountain Home, Boise, Shoshone, and Pocatello. Its articles of incorporation suggested that the group would endeavor "to promote closer unity and companionship among its members. Promote Americanizm [sic]. To encourage and aid all alien members desirous of becoming citizens of the United States of America by Naturalization to Citizenship." The organization also produced Spanish editions of the United States Constitution and the manual of the Daughters of the American Revolution. One study documented that from 1938 to 1947, 32 percent of the Basque immigrants became citizens, a much higher percentage than in previous decades.[15]

Religiously, they also began to mix, though not entirely by choice. In 1928, only nine years after its opening, the Church of the Good Shepherd was closed by Bishop Edward J. Kelly as an exclusively Basque chapel. An unpublished portion of a history of the Diocese of Boise, written in 1943, asserts that the "Basques were becoming Americanized so quickly that they found they could attend services at [St. John's Cathedral] the same as others." Also, Good Shepherd's income was "not sufficient to warrant the maintenance of a separate parish, especially one within eight blocks of the Cathedral." Others have claimed that Bishop Kelly, the youngest Catholic bishop in the United States at that time, closed the parish because he did not believe in ethnic churches; he also encouraged parishes in Lewiston and Pocatello, both with large Italian populations, to downplay their ethnicity. By 1928 Good Shepherd had become the bishop's private chapel, and though a number of Basque women from the area attended his early-morning masses, most Basques shifted to other parishes. The breakup of their exclusively Basque congregations and their exposure to American Catholicism represented another step toward assimilation.[16]

But the real Americanization was taking place among their U.S.-born children, many of whom were in college or already beginning professional careers. Fewer than 5 percent of the second generation of Basques stayed in sheepherding; the remainder were represented in almost every occupation in the state. Their parents provided not only an education but also a reputation as valued employees, improving employment opportunities for the next generation. Many merchants hired second-generation Basques to attend to foreign-born Basque customers. Ironically, jobs they acquired because of their Basque heritage simultaneously drew them away from Basque culture.[17]

Second-generation Basques in Idaho were beginning to determine, as their parents had, to what degree they would take on the ways of America. Some found jobs far away from Idaho, in places where they would enter completely into mainstream U.S. life. Although few Basque immigrants married non-Basques, according to one study about two-thirds of second-generation Basques married non-Basques. Unlike the experience of other ethnic groups in the United States, there is little evidence that immigrant parents disapproved. On the contrary, many parents seemed to relish the Americanization of their children. One American woman wanted to learn Basque cooking to satisfy her husband's appetite for the traditional food he had grown up eating. When she asked her mother-in-law for help, the older woman replied, "You cook American. Johnny eat your food. You no cook Basque, cook American."

Yet it was sometimes a radical shift for second-generation Basques to take spouses with whom their parents could barely communicate. One second-generation Basque man who married a non-Basque woman said, "I do not use the Basque language in my home. But my mother, who has been in this country over thirty-five years, can't speak enough English to converse with my wife and my children. The children have almost no association with their grandmother."[18]

In John Edlefsen's 1940s survey, 97 percent of first-generation Basques said they gave "their full approval" to intermarriage between their children and non-Basques. "My children have their own lives to lead and a happy marriage is the most important thing," one Basque said. "Most important is not whether or not they are Basque, but whether or not they are good people." Another comment was even more revealing of Basque parents' feelings about their children's amalgamation into American society: "They are all Americans and should marry as they choose."[19]

The Americanization of the second generation was apparent to other Idahoans, some of whom had grown up or gone to school with Basques. Non-Basques began to notice the decline of Basque customs in the boardinghouses, in the streets during holidays, and even on the handball courts. "As the second-generation Basques progressed through American schools, their interests shifted to American sports," one author wrote. "The foreign-born became too old for this fast, strenuous game [of handball]. . . . The pelota courts will probably never again resound to the smash of the pelota on concrete walls and to the shouts of the excited spectators." Joseph Harold Gaiser predicted in 1944 that most of the frontons "will probably remain as ruins when the last foreign-born pelota player has passed away."[20]

At social gatherings Basques still honored traditions, but for many of the second generation, the methods had changed. Journalist Jack Beardwood wrote in 1937: "With the exception of a few Basque celebrations, the young Basques attend American social functions. . . . Basque dances which used to be a regular treat for Boise residents, are no longer held, except on special occasions." A Boise sociologist found that while almost all immigrants knew Basque dances, a third of the second generation did not. They learned to dance to American music at high school formals and other social occasions, and doing a jota or another traditional Basque dance could be a challenging venture. There was no formal instruction for Basque dancing, one Basque claimed, so "you'd just watch someone and try to go out there and do it." (But, he added, "only if you were lit up a little bit.") One Basque author lamented that during Basque holidays, "the younger Basques enter into the dances, but they are losing the poise and the rhythm. They have forgotten the purpose of the celebration. They are interested in a good time."[21]

They had grown up in Basque homes, speaking Basque, hearing Basque music, eating Basque food, but their years in American schools, American neighborhoods, and American churches changed them. Later in life, a few might try to relearn long-forgotten Basque vocabulary or improvise dance steps, but by the 1930s most second-generation Basques—consciously or not—had moved into the almost irreversible pattern of American living. One Basque immigrant in Idaho acknowledged this change in his children: "Their lives have been such that they could never orient themselves to the life and customs of the Basques, particularly in Europe," he said. "They would not be considered Basques in Spain."[22]

7

Wartime: A Point of Departure

The Spanish Civil War

By the 1930s Basque immigrants returning to their hometowns for visits might have been astonished at the changes. After Sabino Arana died, his Basque nationalist followers worked steadily to spread propaganda about their movement, and the Basque Nationalist Party received an increasing share of the representation to the Cortes, the Spanish parliament. Basque nationalists hungry for autonomy even sent a delegation to the peace negotiations in Versailles, France, at the close of World War I; their requests for aid from the victorious Big Four, however, were rejected.[1]

Interest in Basque culture continued to thrive even as the political situation in Spain grew increasingly turbulent in the 1920s and 1930s. After 1923, when Spanish general Miguel Primo de Rivera established a military dictatorship adamantly opposed to separatism, the nationalist movement survived it, spreading into uncharted areas of Gipuzkoa. By 1930 there were two hundred *batzokiak*, the Basque centers that Sabino Arana had founded, and the country witnessed a renaissance in the study of Basque language, music, folklore, and participation in Basque sports.[2]

Nationalists' political activity further intensified when Alfonso XIII abdicated the throne in April 1931, initiating the Second Spanish Republic—a loose confederation of the regions of Spain. The republic embraced a wide spectrum of ideologies, including Socialist, Communist, and Anarchist parties, and it immediately presented a difficult decision for the Basques. Elements of the republic were strongly antichurch, which was unacceptable to conservative Catholic Basques; the republic, however, offered nationalists their strongest chance for self-government, and they drafted an Autonomy Statute, which gave them more independence than they had had since the end of the First Carlist War in 1839. But once again Basques were destined to divide among themselves; both Araba and Navarre rejected draft versions of the Autonomy Statute.

In the summer of 1936 the four regions split even more radically, as did all of Spain.[3] On July 19, 1936, a group of Spanish military leaders, including General Francisco Franco, led a rebellion against the republic. By the end of that day the capital cities of Araba and Navarre were in the hands of the rebel military units under the command of General Emilio Mola. The Basque Nationalist Party in Bizkaia and Gipuzkoa made the decision to back the forces of the republic, though they were clearly choosing the lesser of two evils. The Basques, in some respects, had more in common with Franco's Nationalists. They shared devotion to the Catholic Church and adherence to social order. Although the Republican government had promised full autonomy to the Basque regions, the decision to join their side was still a blind leap. It was later claimed that up to one-third of the population of Bizkaia supported the rebels under Franco.[4]

In late July Mola's troops pushed north from Navarre toward Donosti, the capital of Gipuzkoa, in an effort to cut off the two Republican Basque regions. With their superior artillery the rebels reached the Gipuzkoan city of Irun, which by that time had been almost completely destroyed by fire, and on September 13 Mola's forces took Donosti without firing a shot. That left Bizkaia as the sole Basque fortress against the rebels, and rendered meaningless the October 1 passage of the Basque Autonomy Statute. On October 7 the municipal councilors of Bizkaia chose José Antonio de Aguirre as the first Basque president, and he stood beneath the Tree of Gernika to take his oath of office. At the same moment Mola's troops were only twenty-five miles away, preparing for their final surge into Bilbao.[5]

Aguirre had taken command of a sinking ship. Gipuzkoa was lost, and thousands of refugees poured into the already crowded Bilbao, yet the new president decided to throw all energies into the defense of the city. The Basque government began a heavy recruiting program, calling up Bizkaian men to the front by bus, car, or bicycle. Later that fall, there were about forty infantry battalions of 600 to 750 men each, toting all manner of weapons, from hunting rifles to mining explosives. Although poorly trained militarily, many Basques had been hardened by their lives of labor in the nearby mountains. On the day before a rebel push across the Gipuzkoan border, arms arrived from Germany to help the Basques repulse the charge. (Ironically, it was German military power that would contribute to the Basques' defeat.)[6]

The defense of Bilbao required strict rationing, and many Basques went for long stretches of time eating nothing but garbanzos. Aguirre also concentrated on building a network of fortifications around the city called the Cinturón de Hierro (the Belt of Iron). He ordered fifteen thousand workers and architects to construct the two-hundred-kilometer fortification, a Basque version of the Maginot Line laced with barbed wire and cement machine-gun bunkers. The Cinturón de Hierro was about 40 percent complete by March when disaster struck; the officer who had designed and supervised it deserted to the rebel side, taking the fortification's plans with him. He gave the rebels information on the weak points of the Cinturón and the exact number of weapons in the Basque arsenal. By late March Mola was more than ready to begin his spring offensive, a last push into Bilbao.[7]

The rebels began the attack from the air, showering bombs on the industrial town of Durango with the aid of 120 aircraft of the German Condor Legion. They dropped leaflets over Bilbao with a message from Mola: "If submission is not immediate I will raze [Bizkaia] to the ground, beginning with the industries of war. I have the means to do so." It was the prelude to an even worse disaster for the town of Gernika. On Monday, April 26, 1937—market day when farmers in the area brought their produce to town—the Condor Legion raided Gernika for three hours, destroying almost all buildings with explosives and incendiary bombs and mowing down unarmed people with machine guns. When the attack was over, 1,645 people had been killed and 889 wounded—many of them relatives and friends of Basques who had moved to Idaho. It was history's first aerial attack on civilians. Years later at the Nuremberg war crimes trials, Hermann Goering, the chief of the German Luftwaffe, admitted that the attack had been a rehearsal for Nazi aerial bombardment tactics.[8]

Within a week Mola's troops, alongside two Italian divisions, advanced toward Bilbao. All Basque forces had abandoned the stations of the Cinturón, rendering the deserter's information irrelevant as Mola pushed beyond the fortification for a final assault on Bilbao on June 2. Defeat was inevitable. Basques frantically tried to evacuate the city by sea and find safety in France and England or join Basque communities in Argentina and Venezuela. Late on the afternoon of June 19 a brigade of soldiers from Navarre raised the monarchist flag over Bilbao's city hall, symbolizing the victory of the rebel forces over the Basques.[9]

Thousands of Basque troops retreated westward to join the Republican forces in the Spanish region of Santander. Italian forces pushed westward as well, however, and exhausted remnants of the Basque army gathered at the port of Santoña to surrender. On August 24 Basque leaders and Italian representatives of the rebel forces signed the Pact of Santoña. The Basques agreed to surrender all weapons, while the Italians promised to protect the lives of Basque soldiers and to allow the departure of Basque officials. But within days, most surrendering Basques were handed over to the Spanish and moved to concentration camps or the nearby Deusto Prison. The rebels disregarded the Pact of Santoña and tried the Basque prisoners without legal defense, declaring them guilty of "armed rebellion." Many were summarily executed. The rest were given long prison terms at Deusto, where conditions "def[ied] description." The rebels crammed groups of forty prisoners into cells of less than thirty square yards with no running water or toilet facilities. Prisoners lived on tiny portions of bread and soup. They were forced to sing the Spanish national anthem and were beaten if they refused.[10]

After capturing Bilbao, rebels began almost immediately to eradicate all signs of Basque identity. They confiscated private property and took over factories for weapons production. Teachers were fired immediately unless they could prove that they had been neutral during the war. Hundreds of Basques, including sixteen priests who had served as Basque chaplains, were taken to the countryside or to graveyards to be executed. Yet, while they were massacring Basque priests, Franco's rebels were being celebrated as "the savior" of the Catholic Church in Spain. On August 28, the same day Basques were shipped to concentration camps in a betrayal of the Pact of Santoña, the pope recognized Franco's government as the legal regime of Spain. Hundreds of Basque priests and monks were imprisoned or transported to other parts of the country.[11]

The Franco regime also attempted to erase Basque culture forever. The Basque language was prohibited in all public places, and those speaking Euskera on the street were jailed. In birth, marriage, and death registries Basque names were replaced with Spanish equivalents, and even Basque names on tombstones were scratched off. At the conclusion of the Spanish Civil War, in 1939, Franco ordered soldiers to confiscate the property of all leftist party members or Republican soldiers. This command left thousands of Basques impoverished.[12]

But instead of extinguishing Basque identity, the war and Franco's subsequent severity unified the Basques. As Robert P. Clark wrote, "One old soldier from those days told me that he first felt that he was Basque, and, therefore, different from the Spanish, on the day he stood with his battalion in the plaza in Bilbao before the Hotel Carlton, where the Basque government had its headquarters, and heard President Aguirre exhort them to [the] defense of their homeland." It was the kind of experience that many Basques in Idaho would never have— a dramatic point of departure for those who suffered the Spanish Civil War's tragedies from the other side of the Atlantic.[13]

An Agonizing Time

For Basques who had moved to Idaho, the Spanish Civil War presented a series of painful choices. Hearing of the outbreak of war in the summer of 1936, and knowing that the violence directly endangered the lives of loved ones back home, they felt helpless. They scanned newspapers and listened to the radio for news of the war's developments. One Basque from Mountain Home recalled the tension of those early months: "I can vividly remember how those of us here in the American-Basque community would wait anxiously for the mail to see who would be the next recipient of those traditional letters, edged in black, announcing another death in the homeland." It was an agonizing time for most, thousands of miles away from relatives and friends who had been thrust from the periphery directly into the center of historical events.[14]

Although the Spanish Civil War was widely covered by the press, it was often difficult for the Idaho Basques to receive news about the fate of their hometowns. Joe Eiguren, who had moved to the United States in 1934 to herd sheep, grew tired of the isolation on the range and subscribed to *La Prensa*, a Spanish newspaper published in New York. Though the newspaper often arrived three weeks late, it allowed him to follow world events, especially the war in Spain. One day in mid-May 1937, as he sat in the foothills of the Owyhee Mountains skimming his latest copy, an article written by a French journalist caught his attention. It was an account of the bombing of Gernika. "I felt like I was in a trance," he recalled. Several of his friends worked in Gernika, just twenty-two miles from his hometown, Lekeitio. "I remember reading the account . . . 'Here I am surrounded by these Basque women, hysterically crying, bleeding, with their hands steaming after digging in the ashes to look for their loved ones.'" Joe Eiguren felt helpless, stuck in the hills alone, wondering for weeks which of his friends had been killed in the bombing. "I didn't even know where I was. That's my recollection of Gernika. All I could see was those poor young women looking for something that wasn't going to be there."[15]

But despite the war's tragedies, Basques in Idaho were reluctant to throw their support behind the war cause, let alone to return to Euskadi and fight. Most had emigrated long before nationalist passion had spread to rural areas, and as one Basque scholar claimed, they might have viewed the cause as "a failed utopian idea." A fiercely anti-Republican press in the United States depicted Basques as defending "red separatists," slanting many Americans' views toward Franco's Nationalists. The Catholic hierarchy in the United States also backed Franco as the slayer of the forces of communism. One Idahoan recalled the nuns in his Catholic elementary school classroom leading the children in prayers for Franco's troops.[16]

It created an agonizing situation for Basques in Idaho. They feared the communist label yet still wanted to support family and friends in the Basque Country. Most chose a middle path. Already disdainful of politics, they avoided official support of the Basque war effort but scrambled to send money to help their families survive the ravages of war. If they took any collective action, it was mostly for humanitarian aid. In the summer of 1937 the *Idaho Statesman* reported: "Gaiety at [a Basque picnic] may be sobered somewhat by the reason underlying the gathering. Proceeds from the affair will be sent to the Basque region of Spain to care for Basque children orphaned by the current Spanish Civil War." Basques in Boise also used the proceeds from a dance later that year to buy one thousand blankets for Basque women prisoners of war. Such efforts allowed Idaho Basques to help their families in Euskadi without appearing to be zealous communist members of the Spanish Republic.[17]

While eager to provide humanitarian aid, Basques hesitated when approached by the cash-strapped Basque government. In December 1937 Ramón de la Sota, the official Basque delegate to the United States, visited Boise to provide information and raise money for the Basque war effort. During his ten-day stay, he met with local Basque and American leaders, attended Basque parties, and along with another delegate challenged Boise's best handball players in a fund-raising match at Anduiza's fronton. Hungry for war news, Basques turned out in large numbers at the events and warmly welcomed the delegation. But, according to one local Basque, "[There] was lots of moral support—but not much financial." Sota's fund-raising was unsuccessful.[18]

After the war the Basque government, now in exile, tried again to raise support from the Basque community in the American West. But Idaho Basques proved even less enthusiastic now than they had been during the war. They were either unaware of or unconcerned about Franco's efforts to destroy Basque culture and to integrate the region with the Spanish state. This lack of support became glaringly apparent after the Basque delegation in New York decided to open a subdelegation office in Boise. The downtown office was run by Juan Bilbao, who had accompanied Sota on his unsuccessful 1937 visit. The office was fronted to be "of a completely cultural character" and would also "serve to encourage Basques to become American citizens." The *Boise Capitol News* wrote that, according to Bilbao, "a second aim of the office here is to find relatives and friends of Boise's Basques who have migrated to other countries as refugees and who have not been heard from since their migration."[19]

But the subdelegation had political motives as well. In a letter to one of the few strong Basque nationalists in Idaho, Bilbao encouraged the stirring of political interest: "Little by little, and with much tact, talk to [Basques]—always men—to see if you can form a group loyal to the Basque Nationalist Party." But Bilbao soon realized that few political or financial objectives could be met. Paralleling the experience of Sota's failure to gain financial support, Bilbao closed the office when he saw little hope of awakening political interest.[20]

Even after the war, Basques in Idaho still felt compelled to distance themselves from communism and display their loyalty to America. In November 1940 William K. Hart, the president of the Independent Order of Spanish-Basque Speaking People of Idaho, Inc., issued a rare press statement denying allegations that Basques in Idaho espoused communism. "The Basque people throughout the entire United States clearly and fully realize the third international communist party, headed by Stalin, methodically fomented the recent Spanish Civil War." He claimed that the war "kept our people in a blood bath for three long years," resulting in the deaths of one million people. All Americans, he said, should face the cold realization that "the one and only purpose of the Communist Party here in the United States is to destroy our American way of government and to make our United States of America a republic of Soviet Russia."[21]

Basques in Idaho were committed to living in their new country. They had their own families and responsibilities in the United States. Boosting the Basque cause in Euskadi was a much lower priority. They had not suffered the tragedies of the war and its aftermath, the events that solidified Basque unity in Euskadi. While their friends and relatives were experiencing the repression of Franco's rule, Basques in Idaho were having their own unique experiences. "Why should we get involved in things over there?" one Basque woman in Idaho said about the Spanish Civil War. "We have plenty to do for our own soldiers, for our own country." In the coming years, Basques would be doing more for their new country than they ever imagined.[22]

Basques and World War II

The United States became a different place almost immediately after the Japanese attack on Pearl Harbor. The nation unified quickly and concentrated all its efforts on winning the war; oftentimes even ethnic differences were brushed aside as the United States faced a common enemy. Movies showed men of Italian, Irish, Polish, and British descent wearing the same American uniform. This common war experience was the central event that shaped American national identity for that generation.[23]

The war also unified and Americanized Basques in Idaho. "During World War II, there was a feeling among everyone that we were pulling together," said one Basque woman, whose husband enlisted immediately after Pearl Harbor. Even Basques born in the Old Country, who only a few years earlier had been hesitant to get involved in a war fought near their own hometowns, rallied to the American war cause. The harmonizing effect most dramatically influenced American-born second-generation Basques, who passed through this common American experience with millions of others of their age group. Joe Eiguren had spent the majority of his life in the Basque Country, but he recalled that when he heard of the attack on Pearl Harbor, he grew passionate about fighting for the United States. "Right then and there I made up my mind I was going to quit herding sheep and join the U.S. military." Even though he was initially rejected at the navy recruiting office in Boise for his lack of proficiency in English, six weeks later he received a letter from the office of Franklin Delano Roosevelt. "I was very happy, and eager, to be a member of our armed services. I was drafted!"[24]

He was not alone among Basques. At least 350 Idaho Basques, both European- and American-born, served in the United States armed forces during World War II. Though the Spanish Civil War had failed to ignite their passion, after Pearl Harbor Basques in Idaho were eager to sacrifice and perhaps even die for America. In 1945, shortly before the conclusion of the war, a local newspaper claimed that at least eight Idaho Basques had been killed in the war, and that fifteen others were missing in action.[25]

Even some Basques who were ineligible for the draft joined the Idaho reserves, forming the Basque Company of the Ada County Volunteers. Approved by Idaho's governor, the Basque Company was to provide civil defense against a possible attack on the American mainland. The forty-five men of the Basque volunteers, of which half had been born in the Basque Country, were commanded by Zenon Yzaguirre and had paid for their own uniforms and guns. The *Idaho Statesman* reported in December 1942: "A hard-hitting outfit of riflemen who learned marksmanship on the open range joined up recently with the Idaho volunteer reserves—the state's first all-Basque contingent and probably the only [one] of its kind in the nation." Their commander said the outfit of "dark-eyed, black-haired sons of the Pyrenees" was "not Main Street target shooters, but I'll match them against any riflemen in the world out on the open range or in the mountains." The newspaper praised them as "rugged," "adept military pupils," and "enthusiastic recruits" who "take their training seriously."[26]

"We didn't have a prayer," one of the Basque volunteers recalled years later, laughing. "Thank God no one did attack us. But at the time, it was pretty serious." They were disciplined about their drills, which they continued until the end of the war, though they were never called up. "We trained once a week down by the Riverside Dance Hall," another volunteer recalled. "We worked with firearms and [practiced] what to do in an emergency. A few times we marched in parades."[27]

Basque women also contributed to the American war effort. Some helped the Red Cross by sewing or rolling bandages. One Basque woman said, "I help Red Cross indirectly. I get no credit, but God will give me credit. I help Americans to find mistakes in their knitting. . . . That's my job [in this war]: to help indirect. And I don't mind it." The *Idaho Statesman* heaped praise on the efforts of the women: "Basque girls, renowned in Idaho for their dark-haired beauty, are working hard as U.S.O. hostesses and as nurses' [aides] in hospitals."[28]

The Basque community in Idaho helped the war cause financially as well. In December 1944, after a successful fund-raising dance, Idaho Basques presented a check for $2,027.40 to the Red Cross. Spurred by a national drive, the Basques pledged to buy $1 million in war bonds; by February 1945 they had purchased $668,000 worth. Purchasing bonds offered Basques the perfect opportunity to demonstrate their loyalty to America while staying within their ethnic group—and making money. "What if buying does mean sacrifice?" one Basque asked at the time. "Is this not our America, the greatest land, that needs the money? The Basques do their best. We are buying bonds as part of America, not just as Basques." One newspaper stated that they had bought so many bonds because "90 percent of the 5,000 Basques in southwestern Idaho are loyal American citizens by birth or naturalization."[29]

World War II represented another dramatic point of departure for Basques in Idaho. The first generation felt proud to contribute to the effort. Sharing the sacrifices of war gave them a common American experience. Basques suffered the same fears as other Americans, worrying about the lives of their sons, husbands, and friends in the armed forces. At the conclusion of the war they rejoiced with the rest of the country, feeling that they, too, had played a small role in the victory. Basques in Idaho had already been engaged in Americanization; the war simply accelerated the process.

8

A Subculture Is Born

Mirroring the experiences of other immigrant groups, second-generation Basques grew up in a hyphenated world, raised at home with Old World traditions and language but exposed on the outside to English, football, proms, and American popular culture. Most had finished high school, and some continued on to universities. Consciously or not, each second-generation Basque was choosing how he or she would enter the American mainstream. Some left Idaho, fully integrating into modern U.S. life. Others stayed and maintained parts of the culture of their parents. In the process they helped create a subculture unique to both Euskadi and the United States.

This subculture actually began with the immigrant generation. Second-generation children were often influenced by the celebrations they attended with their parents in boardinghouses or private homes, dazzled by the boisterous singing and intricate dance steps. "There are certain things in the Basque culture that are a lot more pleasant than the U.S. culture," said one second-generation Basque woman, recalling parties and dances on Boise's Grove Street. "In the Basque culture, there was a lot more fun and a great sense of community." Pete Cenarrusa acquired an early respect for the Basque culture at his parents' ranch in Carey. "To me, being around Basques gave me a great deal of security," he said. "I felt good, just from the image of the Basques getting together. I enjoyed sitting in these Basque rooming houses, where they got together and played *mus.* . . . I was able to study them and, in some ways, become part of them."[1]

As they passed into adulthood, many of the second generation reserved at least part of their lives for Basque customs or social events. In 1936 a group of young second-generation Basque women began to gather occasionally at a downtown clothing store. They formed the Basque Girls Club and held regular meetings, usually at a member's home. The women volunteered for community service and rolled bandages for the Red Cross in World War II. During their meetings they exchanged news in both Basque and English. "We start out in English," a member said at the time, "then just fall into [Basque]. Habit, I guess. It's easier. . . . We're all Americans first, you understand, but we are proud of our Basque heritage, too." The group continued to meet into the 1990s, and though many members were octogenarians, the name of the organization remained the Basque Girls Club.[2]

Others of the second generation were captivated by Basque music and dance, and they picked up lessons from their parents or other Basque immigrants. Angela Larrinaga began to take accordion lessons from her father at age fifteen, eventually becoming competent enough to play at boardinghouse dances. Another second-generation Basque, Jimmy Jausoro, would make Basque music an even bigger part of his life. Born in Nampa in 1920, he grew up in his parents' boardinghouse, the Spanish Hotel. Like most boardinghouse children, he was put to work at an early age, fetching soup bones from the butcher shop, cleaning the brass spittoons, and scrubbing the floor on his knees every Saturday. It was not all work. He enjoyed himself at the Spanish Hotel's dances and was particularly amazed by the flashy accordion playing of one of the boarders. He decided then to start saving for his own accordion—not an easy-to-reach goal for a thirteen year old during the depth of the Depression.[3]

One day, "when nobody was looking," he slid a quarter down the Spanish Hotel's slot machine and—"ching, ching, ching . . . jackpot!" exclaimed Jimmy, remembering his joy years later. The money helped him buy his first accordion, for $120, a shiny new Hohner with mother-of-pearl keys. Determined to master it, he picked up tips from boarders and took lessons for a while, slinging the accordion over his back and riding his bicycle one-handed to his teacher's house. After learning a few songs, he began to play in Nampa's pool halls, setting out a hat for nickels and dimes; as he got better, he sat in with other musicians at Basque dances and became popular in the Basque community. "There was always Jimmy," another musician recalled. "He was everybody's favorite guy on the block."[4]

By the late 1930s there was no shortage of Basque occasions at which he and other musicians could play. One such occasion was the Sheepherders' Ball. Though it would become one of the most celebrated Basque social events in Idaho, the Sheepherders' Ball was actually created during a row between insurance groups. In 1928 Boise Basques formed a second mutual aid society, La Fraternidad Vasca Americana, which rivaled the established La Sociedad de Socorros Mutuos. Many Basques encouraged the benefits of consolidation, which as one Basque man suggested would have created "one hell of an outfit." But, he added, "three Basques get together and no two will agree. There was keen competition between the groups. They hated each other."[5] At meetings to consider consolidation, "they couldn't keep any order, any semblance of a meeting. Just a contest to see who could talk the loudest over the top of each other." Both organizations scheduled Christmas dances for herders in town on the same night. The influential sheepman John Archabal mediated the controversy and convinced the two sides to organize one dance with a lamb auction for charity. Both parties agreed, and the annual Sheepherders' Ball became a mainstay in Boise and, later, in other southern Idaho towns.[6]

The Sheepherders' Ball became known as an "apron and overalls" dance, because admission required sheepherder garb or traditional Basque costumes. Sometimes a stand was set up near the door, where any partygoers who arrived inappropriately dressed could buy jeans on the spot. Although it was reserved for Basques and their guests, the Sheepherders' Ball attracted the attention of the general public. On December 19, 1936, the *Boise Capitol News* wrote: "Black-eyed sons and daughters of the Pyrenees danced their beloved 'jota' with snapping fingers and nimble feet Friday evening at the annual Basque Sheepherders' Ball held at Danceland, to the music of Benito Arrego's accordion and pandareen." Symbolic of the acculturating forces for this generation, one observer said, "Basque musicians, playing the Old World tunes, can be heard at one end of the hall at the same time an American orchestra is playing at the other end."[7]

In the early 1930s the American-Basque Fraternity organized a picnic in Boise on the Fourth of July for all Basques, and it, too, became a tradition. Later organized by the women's Organisación Independiente Sociale, the picnic was switched to the last weekend of July, near the July 31 feast day of the Basque saint, Ignatius of Loyola. Again, Basque communities in smaller towns organized their own summer picnics, annual events in which Basques could dance the jota and sing traditional songs—but also toss baseballs and compete in gunnysack races.[8]

The "New" Sheepherders

It was clear that most Basque immigrants, when given an opportunity, left the occupation that had been responsible for their success in the state—sheepherding. Nevertheless, despite the immigration quotas, a fresh supply of Basques made their way into American society via the sheep industry. The great respect that Basques commanded in the industry was most prominently illustrated by a series of laws created to help Basques sidestep immigration quotas. By the 1940s there was a severe labor shortage in the sheep industry, partially caused by the drain of labor into the war effort. Desperate to retain reliable Basque employees, western sheep owners pleaded with their government representatives to help grant residency to Basques who had entered the country illegally. The movement led to what has been called the "Sheepherders' Laws," which granted residency to hundreds of Basque men in Idaho and paved the way for the legal entry of hundreds more in the following decades.[9]

Joining the efforts of other western members of Congress, Idaho U.S. senator Henry Dworshak in 1947 wrote a letter to an immigration official requesting that a group of Basque sheepherders be allowed to stay in the country, because they were "well qualified and exceptional" workers. In the 1950s Senator Frank Church also requested the Judiciary Committee to consider a bill to help thirteen Basques achieve citizenship. "In Idaho," he wrote the committee chairman, "we do not look at immigrant Basques as foreigners but as Idahoans. They have contributed much to Idaho's culture, its economy and its history." Other members of Idaho's congressional delegation, including Representative—later Senator—James McClure, would create legislation for Basques to stay in the country.[10]

Nevertheless, sheepmen seemed perpetually short of workers in the middle decades of the century. In 1952 the *Idaho Wool Growers Bulletin* wrote: "The Western sheep industry . . . must have ample labor. There is [*sic*] not sufficient numbers of persons willing and qualified to supply present needs. Regrettably American labor prefers town jobs at less pay and will not work with sheep. . . . The simple solution to the problem is for Congress to raise the limits restricting importation"—which is exactly what it did. Nevada Senator Patrick McCarran was influential in pushing through Congress special immigration provisions for Basques. The agreements allowed Basque herders to emigrate to the United States on three-year contracts, renewable if the herder temporarily left the country when the contract expired. Later the government allowed herders to apply for permanent residence when they had completed their three-year contract. Hundreds of Basques immigrated to Idaho under the provisions of this legislation.[11]

These new immigrants, however, came under circumstances that were different from those of earlier decades. Most came by airplane, guided every step of the way, and their contracts guaranteed them salaries for at least three years. They enjoyed the benefits of the communities that were established by the hundreds of first- and second-generation Basques who had been in Idaho for decades. Their upbringing in the Basque Country was also different from the experience of earlier Basque immigrants. They had suffered the agony of living in the Basque Country under Franco's dictatorship—the social and economic woes that had shaped a new identity for Basques in Euskadi. "Nationalism took a boom as big as an atomic bomb after Franco came to power," one later immigrant said. "To me being Basque is the biggest thing in my life, because that's all I learned from the time I was four or five: 'Gora Euskadi Askatuta!' [Long Live the Independent Basque Country!] The people that came over prior to [the Spanish Civil War] didn't learn that because they didn't have the Franco experience." In future years, this difference in experience would become glaring in the Idaho Basque community.[12]

The sheepherders who came after 1950 struggled with many of the same hardships as their predecessors had, but time had granted them some advantages. Their camps were more accessible, and they received more visitors than did herders of earlier decades. By 1955 they would even have the Catholic sacraments brought to them by Father Francisco

Aldasoro. Basques in the Boise area took up a collection to buy the priest a new car so he could make his rounds. To ease their solitude, sheepherders would listen to the radio, which by 1950 offered a weekly program in the Basque language on KDSH. Julian Lachiondo was the first Basque to offer the program, and he used his stack of records from the Old Country, which he played every week. Cecil Jayo took his turn for a year, and by the late 1950s Espe Alegria took his place on KBOI, a Boise radio station with a signal powerful enough to reach Canada and Mexico. The *Idaho Statesman* later reported: "Many a Basque sheep camp quieted as the herders listened to music that reminded them of the singing and dancing at the fiestas for the patron saint of their villages." Speaking only in Basque, Alegria presented sports scores, played requests for songs, and wished listeners *Zorionak* [Happy Birthday]. "No matter where I was, I had to listen to [Espe's program]," said one former herder. "I really enjoyed that." Espe Alegria's KBOI *Basque Program* continued until 1981.[13]

Earlier Basque immigrants came to Idaho and immediately found clusters of boardinghouses, but the latecomers encountered a whole new community forming in the state by the 1950s. Even though the sheepherding work was still drudgery for most of them, they came to a society in which they were already respected for being honorable hard workers. They left a setting where their culture was under attack and moved to a new one where some of their customs, though changed by American influence, still survived.

A Choice of Preservation

Basques in Europe did not have boardinghouses, the Basque Girls Club, the Sheepherders' Ball, or Basque picnics. Basque immigrants were playing the old songs and dancing the customary steps, but they were doing it in a new context, in the dining rooms of boardinghouses, on the porches of their Basque friends, or by picnic tables at the Mode Country Club. Few of their children had been to the Basque Country, and the Basque culture that they inherited was gathered in bits and pieces at impromptu dances and parties, far from heavily researched. It was rural Basque life transferred to an American setting, and it resulted in some adaptation. Like a story whispered through a series of ears, Basque culture was subject to changes in its new surroundings—pieces were added and dropped, and what came out was often quite different from the original source.

Without opportunities to view Basque society themselves, second-generation Basques often created one, sometimes even borrowing from Spanish tradition. In a 1928 *Idaho Statesman* Sunday feature, second-generation Basque dancers appeared in Andalusian flamenco costumes. "They didn't know what the Basque costume was at that time," one Basque said later. "So when they were asked to dance, they just put that together." While the flamenco example was an extreme, many Basque Americans and Anglo-Americans in general drew little distinction between what was Basque and what was clearly not. The *Boise Capitol News* reported that at one Sheepherders' Ball in the 1930s, "pretty Señora Ruiz of Nampa" performed three Spanish dances and songs, "dressed in elaborate Spanish costumes of lace mantilla, embroidered shawl and tall golden comb."[14]

Yet they tried to preserve what they could. Joseph Harold Gaiser wrote in 1944: "One Basque is brought from Nevada to assist at the [Sheepherders' Ball] since he, alone, recalls the intricacies of several dances." As part of a festival celebrating the centennial of Fort Boise, Basques in Boise gave a temporary Basque farmhouse facade to a downtown boardinghouse. Small groups of dancers assembled for Idaho cultural events. At Boise's annual Music Week in 1938, two young Basque women improvised a traditional costume for a brief dancing exhibition. In 1940 Cipri and Julia Barroetabena organized a Basque dance group in Emmett. The group, which included eight girls, nine boys, and one *txistu* (Basque flute) player, performed at the Idaho State Fair, but the coming of World War II disbanded the group. These early efforts were fleeting, and traditional Basque dancing seemed to be headed for extinction.[15]

This changed under the initiative of Juanita "Jay" Hormaechea, who thought dancing was too important for the Basque community in Idaho to lose. Growing up and working in Boise's Basque boardinghouses early in the century, she learned Basque dances at a young age. Like many of her generation, she enjoyed the regular Sunday dances, which she continued to attend even after she was no longer employed as a maid. Though immigration quotas and a sheep industry slowdown cut off the flow of Basques into Idaho, Boise's boardinghouses remained full, the celebrations as lively as ever. In 1947 at a dance in Nampa's

Spanish Hotel, "I was dancing with a group of sheepherders," she re-called. "And in those days, they would grab those girls around the waist and lift them up. (Boys were tickled to death to grab you, anyway, you know.)" She admonished them for not dancing correctly: "'That isn't the way to dance that, now quit it!' 'Well, show us how to dance, then,' they said. From there, I had an idea." She decided to teach young Basques in the area to dance the traditional steps. She asked Jimmy Jausoro and another Basque musician, Domingo Ansotegui, if they would play accordion and tambourine at her lessons, and they agreed. Jimmy and Domingo would provide dancers with music for the next thirty-seven years.[16]

Her classes started in early 1948 at the Western Square Dance Hall on the second floor of a building in the Hyde Park neighborhood of north Boise. Word of the classes had circulated, and about forty children showed up for the first lesson. Jay stepped in front and broke down the steps of the jota in a method repeated for decades: "Side . . . kick . . . one, two, three! . . . Side . . . kick . . . one, two, three!" Some children, especially the boys, were reluctant participants. One of her pupils, Albert Erquiaga, remembered that he and his friends refused to try the steps. "We would not do it. Jay could not get us out there." In the end Jay won, and one by one her students came out to the wooden floor and struggled through their first jotas.[17]

That first class had implications that few realized. Most essentially, it represented one of the first organized efforts to preserve Basque traditions in Idaho. Until then, traditions had been practiced by the immigrants who brought them, then enjoyed in fleeting moments by their children. Through her lessons, hundreds of children who otherwise might have strayed away from the culture were exposed to Basque dancing. One Basque man said years later, "[Jay Hormaechea] did things that other people would not have tried. A lot of us followed, but I'm not sure many of us would have . . . without her doing it first." A 1948 *Idaho Statesman* article was prophetic: "If the fiery jota is danced for years to come by members of the Basque colony in Boise and the Boise valley, it will be partly because a slim, handsome, brown-eyed Basque woman is determined that the dance shall not be forgotten."[18]

She kept instructing, with the help of Jimmy Jausoro, Domingo Ansotequi, Angela Larrinaga, and other volunteer musicians. Attendance fluctuated—sometimes fewer than ten children stood behind her—but after a few months most students learned the basics of the jota and its second part, the *porrusalda*. The Sunday lessons became a habit, a gathering day for all ages that continued long after Boise's last boarding-house closed.

The lessons drew attention. A local newspaper reported: "Every Sunday evening exciting accordion and tambourine music with Spanish accents echoes from the [Western] hall, where [Jay Hormachea] leads a class of younger generation Basques through the intricate steps of 'La Jota.'" Early in 1949 the organizational committee for Music Week, Boise's annual May performance festival, approached Jay about producing a show of Basque song and dance. She accepted and set out to organize a massive production. Rather than featuring only her young students, she decided to draw on the talents of Basques of all ages. Jay approached different groups and asked them to refine their abilities. Women who had already been singing at gatherings worked out harmonies, jota dancers perfected steps, musicians tightened their songs. "The singing was going on from a long time before [this production]," one of the cast's seven accordionists recalled. "They were taking what people already knew and what people were already doing and bringing it all together to have some kind of a plot."[19]

Preparing for the show was exciting, Angela Larrinaga remembered. "It was the total [Basque] community coming together to put on this program, and there was a unity in the whole area. . . . We used to have these rehearsals every week at one of the ladies' houses, and boy, it was party time! We would sing and we would go over everything until everybody thought it was perfect. Then they would bring out coffee and every imaginable kind of treat. It was just really great."[20]

Under Jay's supervision, *The Song of the Basque* took shape and became one of the most anticipated events of Music Week in 1949. The *Idaho Statesman* estimated that one thousand people attended the dress rehearsal alone. The day of the show, May 9, the newspaper wrote: "For the first time Boise residents will hear a program of native Basque music and dances which will be presented by the Basque 'nation' now centered in southwestern Idaho." More than two thousand crammed into Boise High School auditorium for the show; more than three thousand were turned away at the door. The cast, about two hundred Basques aged three to seventy, waited noisily beneath and around the auditorium's cramped stage, anticipating the eight o'clock curtain.[21]

The narrator, Pete Leguineche, opened by telling the audience, "We feel sincere, heartfelt gratitude to you for taking us into the community and making us a part of you." The curtain then opened with a group of women (listed in the program as Las Bilbanitas) singing in front of a painted countryside scene. They were followed by a jai alai demonstration and three dancing groups, including Jay's youngest dancers. One three-year-old girl, according to the newspaper, "stole the show." With the bright lights and the laughter of the crowd, she lost her place and stopped to look out at the audience. She eventually started up again, "swaying her chubby little hips and swinging her long brown curls. . . . When she took her final bow, somebody else's elbow socked her in the nose." Next were Los Borrachos performing "La Luna Enamora." In the finale, the cast gathered to sing "God Bless America" and its Basque translation, "Gora America." They presented Jay Hormaechea with a bouquet of flowers, its pink ribbon signed in silver ink by the whole cast.[22]

The *Idaho Statesman* praised the performance the following day. "Hundreds thrilled to the greatest Basque spectacle ever seen in the United States at the Music Week performance Monday evening," the review read. "'Song of the Basque' was the greatest night in the Basques' history in America." The production was so popular that it was repeated May 20 to another full house, and a five-record album was made featuring all the music performed in the show.[23]

The success of the Music Week productions created momentum for the Basque community and once again endeared them to Idahoans. "It didn't start everything," one participant said, "but I think 'The Song of the Basque' probably brought the Basque people to the attention of everybody in the Boise valley a little bit more." It was the culmination of the growth of a strong Basque-American community in Idaho. "All of my non-Basque friends were absolutely green with envy," one second-generation Basque said. "They were very envious of the culture, because we were so strong, so close." An editorial praised the efforts of the 1949 Music Week participants: "Were we forced to name our choice [of the best show of the week], we would naturally select Basque night. . . . There is a lesson in the tempo of the Basque, a lesson in the solidity [*sic*] of the race, and a yardstick of its resistance to the present runaway times."[24]

III

The Ethnic Generation

J osie Bilbao, the oldest daughter of Julie and Julio, viewed her Basque background as a benefit, a world away from the kind of discrimination the first Basque immigrants had faced. She especially enjoyed participating in the Oinkaris dance group. "I loved it. The socializing was the best part. It was really a lot of fun to have such a great group of friends, that you got to get together with and go on trips with. If it wasn't for Oinkaris I probably wouldn't have gone to the Basque Country. The precedent was set by so many peers who were older and you respected. Being in Oinkaris has really shaped my life a lot."

Josie went to college at Lewis and Clark in Portland, Oregon. "Being away from the Oinkaris and the whole community, I realized how little I knew about Basques, Basque history, and the political situation. People didn't know anything about Basques, and so to explain it to them you had to know something. . . . It was part of the reason I decided to go to the Basque Country. I needed to go on the program to study and learn on my own." In 1988–89, Josie attended Boise State University's Basque Studies Program in Donosti/San Sebastián. "I was really glad when I started seeing Basque signs on the way from Madrid. And all of a sudden things start getting greener . . . and a lot of the way we romanticize the Basque Country starts coming back to you."

After an extended stay in Euskadi, Josie had a different perspective on parts of the American Basque subculture in Idaho. "Sometimes I was amazed that the dances and things keep going so far from the source. But sometimes it seemed like just a show." What she saw in the States upon her return seemed such a deep contrast to the situation she witnessed in Euskadi, which in many ways was having its own internal debates about Basque nationalism and identity in the post-Franco years, including the debates about the violent activities of ETA. "It's such a major issue in Euskadi that everyone has to decide for themselves, but we [in America] don't. Our situation is such that we don't have to decide if violence is okay to further your cause or preserve your culture. Looking at people making these kinds of decisions made Oinkaris . . . seem like an easy show, like it was easy to put on.

"I also realized . . . that we're very lucky to have this identity that we can jump into or put on, or really study. That it is there for us to pursue in whatever way we want—or just to discard it. But so many of our peers don't even have that to put on, and [I realized] how lucky we are to have that choice."

⇥ ⇤

Anita Bilbao, Julio and Julie's second daughter, joined the Oinkaris also, and like her sister Josie she enjoyed the group, meeting other young Basques who became good friends. But while attending college at Lewis and Clark University in Portland, Oregon, she said, she realized that there were "a lot of other things out there." She decided that she wanted to learn about areas other than the Basque Country, and instead of attending the university program in Euskadi, she traveled to Ecuador. "I feel studying Basque is great, but it really is a limiting area to go into. For me, it's probably going to be important for my kids to speak Spanish or another second language. I want it to be something that's applicable in their lives."

Despite having chosen to travel to Ecuador instead of the Basque Country, Anita Bilbao still felt that being Basque was important to her life. "I think everyone strives so hard to find something within themselves that is meaningful and gives them a link to other people." Basques are "lucky" to have their heritage and community, she said, because many people do not. Sometimes Basque Americans participate "only at festivals, once a summer or a couple times a year. Maybe being Basque is being aware of where other Basques are in the world, or reading about them in the paper. You can express your Basque identity according to your interests—sports, music, food, or maybe your thing is politics, so you read about what's going on [with] ETA. It's a choice you make whether you do these things or not. But I feel it's something that grounds you. You have tradition and people to connect with. Not everyone has that. Even if it is only a small part of your life and you're not really active . . . it is something that's in you and you'll always be a part of."

Anita Bilbao suggested that sometimes pride in Basque ethnicity comes in very small forms. For example, she had acquired a habit from her father. When watching the credits after a movie, she would often look at the list roll down and every once in a while she would see something familiar. She would say to herself, "Hey, that's a Basque name!"

I remember Mom and Josie and Anita would always play around on the *txistu* [Basque flute]," said Amaya Bilbao, the youngest of Julio and Julie's daughters. "And when I was little, I would walk around with a drum in one arm and a *txistu*. I started dancing lessons when I was four." She remembered feeling very impressed with what she learned. She said that she and another Basque friend would "brag about being Basque all the time. . . . We would go around school and act like we knew [how to speak] Basque. Everyone would believe us. We would go around and say the words to these Basque songs rather than sing them, and people thought we were really speaking Basque. And we'd do our little Basque dances out there and say, 'We're *full* Basque.'" She laughed at the memory.

Amaya felt very fortunate to be aware of her Basque background, especially when she realized that so many of her friends were not connected to their heritage. "When I ask people what nationality they are, it seems a lot of people don't even know or don't even care. They have no link at all. . . . That still gets to me. . . . They don't even know anything about their culture. My friends don't make German food, and at our house we make Basque food. I don't speak Basque, but people in my house speak Basque."

╪══ ══╪

Julie and Julio's children felt that growing up in Idaho had exposed them to a large dose of Basque culture. This was not the case for the children of Julio's sister, Dolores, who married a non-Basque man and lived in California. Dolores, her husband, Jim Seielstad, and their children, Andrea, Mark, and Carl, would travel to Boise for occasional visits, and, Andrea Seielstad remembered, "That's when we had the most connection with the Basque culture." She said she often wished she "was all Basque, especially when we came up [to Boise]." She said, laughing, "We were inferior, because we were only half Basque. I remember Carl, my brother, when he was little saying, 'Well, Josie and Anita and Amaya are pedigrees, and we're just mutts.' We're just half-assed Basques." She also said she would often become "kind of jealous" of their cousins in Boise, "because they had the culture here, and they could join Oinkaris, learn the language." Despite living in an area with little exposure to Basque culture, they still felt drawn to their heritage. Mark Seielstad incorporated Basques into his studies of population genetics at Harvard. "I have been sequencing my own DNA. The idea is that since the [Basque] language is different, the people are probably genetically different, maybe there are remnants of an earlier population before them, before expansion into Europe from the Middle East and other places. My study has been inconclusive so far."

For Andrea, there had always been a sense of being part of a unique culture. "I think we identified more strongly with that side of the family than [with] our dad's side; in fact, we don't know that much about our dad's side of the family." Learning the Basque language also interested her. "It seems like if you learn it you're more genuine. You can claim more that you're Basque. Plus, it would be interesting to know. I've thought about learning it," Andrea said, "but I don't have much of an opportunity. . . . I would like to [pass on Basque culture], but I don't know if I have the knowledge."

9

The Oinkari Basque Dancers

At a dance in late 1959 about a dozen young Basques, most of them American-born, made a decision: the next summer, they were all going to go to the Basque Country. With the exception of a young man who had immigrated on a sheepherding contract, none had been there. Some had taken jota instruction from Jay Hormaechea and participated in the Music Week productions, but they had long since quit. Most had finished school or were about to, and a visit to the Basque Country seemed like a good way to celebrate.[1]

The trip "came out of a lark," as one of them later described it, but it would have a dramatic impact on the Basque community in Idaho. It was important not only because it led to the founding of the Oinkari Basque Dancers but also because it initiated so many future trips and symbolized how important a return to roots would become during this time period. "We went to see our families and to see what the Basque Country was like," said Albert Erquiaga. "We went with no intention of dancing or anything like that." They looked at travel brochures and checked into prices. They were surprised to find that the trip was affordable, and in May 1960 eight of them left Boise. One day they ventured to Pasaia, a small Gipuzkoan fishing village, for a festival. They enjoyed the bands that played and saw a demonstration of ram fighting. But they were most "amazed," Albert Erquiaga said, by a group of dancers who, dressed in their street clothes, marched out for an impromptu performance. "It was the first [Basque] dance group we had ever seen." After the performance they met some of the dancers, part of a group called Oinkari, which when translated loosely from Basque means "people who perform with their feet." They invited the Idahoans to attend a more complete performance several days later in France. Intrigued by the Oinkaris' dancing, the Idaho Basques attended several practice sessions. They filmed the sessions and also mapped out the steps on paper.

The night before the Boiseans left the Basque Country, they gathered with the Oinkaris in a small bar in Pasaia. Albert Erquiaga recalled, "We were getting ready to leave and were saying our good-byes. And we wanted to do something for [the Oinkaris] after all they had done for us. One of them said, 'The biggest favor you could do for us would be to go back and start a group and call it Oinkari.'" Toni Achabal, another young Idahoan who made the trip, said years later, "Little did we know then that our group was going to outlive theirs."

This would be difficult, they concluded on the plane back to the United States. Only two men had made the trip and actually seen the dancers, they had neither sheet music nor musicians, and no one had a costume. Nevertheless, determined to follow through on their promise, they recruited male dancers ("hog-tied them," as one later said), studied their notes and films, and talked Jimmy Jausoro into playing accordion for them. They had their first practices in the dance hall of the Basque Center, crawling their way through what they remembered to be the steps and the music. Albert Erquiaga explained, "We would get together and hum the music, and [Jimmy Jausoro] would scratch it down. At the next practice he would have the music written down and say, 'Is this right?' We would listen to it, correct it. That's how we stumbled through it." They watched the films over and over, but some of the steps were still sketchy, so they improvised. One of the dances they enjoyed, *arku* (hoop dance), had been performed by eight men; because of a shortage of male members, the Boise Oinkaris choreographed the dance with four men and four women. Another dance, *jota barri* (new jota), they choreographed on their own. "A lot of our dances were not authentic at all," Toni Achabal said. "They were American-Basque dances."

By that fall, the group had made slow, steady progress, and they announced their first public performance would be at the Sheepherders'

Ball in December. Just as they had with their dance steps, they improvised costumes. The women made their own red satin skirts and bought white stockings and black ballet slippers. The men, unable to acquire the flexible white canvas shoes worn by the dancers in Euskadi, wore street shoes, white shirts, and pants. They borrowed whatever accessories they could find, a sash or a beret. "We didn't coordinate at all," one dancer recalled. They performed during a set break at the dance, held at the Miramar Ballroom, and were greeted by a boisterous crowd. "When we went out to do *arku,* the roar was so loud that we couldn't hear the music," Albert Erquiaga said. Toni Achabal added, "I think people here were so amazed with the idea that a group would go and try something like that. It brought back lots of memories for those folks and lots of tears, too."

After their first performance, the Oinkaris gained dancers and musicians, expanded their repertoire, and attracted attention around the state. By 1962 they were one of five groups to represent the state at the Seattle World's Fair. Their early success stoked excitement among Basques in the area. "There was enthusiasm," Simon Achabal remembered, "not just among the Oinkaris but the whole Basque community, plus the local businesspeople." If the Oinkaris needed to raise money, Basque women would volunteer to prepare fund-raising dinners. The support from the community was even more evident in 1964, when the Oinkaris were invited to be official ambassadors on Idaho Day for the New York World's Fair, the state's sole representation. Although the $22,000 needed to send fifty dancers and musicians seemed prohibitive, local business and professional leaders agreed to help raise funds. "[Idahoans] could see something good happening here," a dancer recalled. "They weren't about to stand in the way of it."[2]

The Oinkaris' trip became somewhat of a statewide quest. Grocery stores like Albertson's invited the group to dance at each of their branches in return for sizable contributions. Borah High School's Spanish and political science clubs combined to donate $96. Three young children from Owyhee County presented the group with a paper sack containing 314 pennies they had saved. The fund-raising was successful. After proclaiming May 23, 1964, Basque Day in Idaho, Governor Robert E. Smylie presented the group with the state flag, telling the Oinkaris, "In raising the money which makes it possible for you to represent the state . . . you carried your art to the people of Idaho and made them a part of your venture. You have added something very worthwhile to Idaho history."[3]

Their performance in New York on Idaho Day was also successful (though the master of ceremonies announced the occasion as "Iowa Day"). On June 18 they traveled to Washington, D.C., performing in the rotunda of a Senate office building. One of the dancers announced the performance with an *irrintzi,* the high-pitched, warbling Basque war cry, which bounced off the walls and attracted the attention of the large lunchtime crowd. The following week, Senator Frank Church of Idaho applauded the Oinkaris in the *Congressional Record* for "thrilling an appreciative audience. . . . Since then, my office has answered numerous questions about this dance group, and about the Basques, a most wonderful people."[4]

Less than four years after their first performance, the Oinkaris had not only helped raise the stature of Basques within Idaho, but also made it known outside the state that parts of Basque culture were thriving in Idaho—something that few states could claim. "There could be no more effective ambassadors for Idaho than this remarkably talented group," the *Idaho Statesman* wrote. "To most people elsewhere in the nation and the world, Idaho conjures up the image of the russet potato. We hope that image never fades. But it's not the kind of picture that lures visitors here, and we can think of no more dramatic way of doing it than through the Basque dancers."[5]

A National Resurgence of Roots

The Oinkaris were caught off guard by their success. "Once it caught on, holy cow! We were dancing every weekend," one member said. They began to receive calls from groups asking for performances in Boise and Sun Valley and for demonstrations at schools and conferences throughout the state. Albert Erquiaga, one of the group's founders, explained, "People were hungry for something like this."[6]

This "hunger" was shared by many, not only in Idaho but throughout the country. There was an awakened interest among Americans in the culture and the history of their ancestors, especially those who were now several generations from the original immigrants. Historian Marcus Lee Hansen proposed a theory for this resurgence, explaining it in simple terms: "What the son [of immigrants] chose to forget, the grandson wishes to remember." Hansen suggested that when an immigrant group reaches the third generation, "an almost irresistible impulse arises," which brings together people from various backgrounds and positions in life because of the "one factor which they have in common—the heritage of blood." Look sixty years past the initial influx of an immigrant group, Hansen said, and you will find more outlets for ethnic expression and study than at any other time. The period from the 1890s until legislation limited entry in 1924 marked the peak of Basque immigration into Idaho. Two generations later, more formal Basque organizations existed than ever before.[7]

This resurgence of roots coincided with one of the most striking periods of social change in American history. From the early 1960s to the late 1970s, a series of events tore the national fabric—the assassinations of John and Robert Kennedy and Martin Luther King Jr., Watergate, and perhaps above all, the Vietnam War, which divided the country as dramatically as World War II had united it. Following one after the other, these incidents shattered American idealism and replaced it with disillusionment and malaise.[8]

Intertwined with these events was disenchantment with the "American Dream." Hippies, minorities, and student groups all attacked the "Establishment" and its failures. They charged the WASP (White Anglo-Saxon Protestant) with forming a cold, alienating society requiring strict WASP credentials for acceptance. Some ethnic groups questioned whether it had been worth giving up their past to adhere to a uniform WASP life. "WASPs have never had to . . . march down Fifth Avenue wearing green," declared one writer at the time. "Every day has been their day in America. No more."[9]

Many stressed the *pluribus* (of many) from the national motto, while discounting the *unum* (one). Many dismissed the assimilation process and argued that cultural pluralism was much more consistent with democratic values. They believed that the country, founded upon individual rights and protection of the minority, should remain consistent by appreciating differences among groups, rather than insisting on a uniform way of life. "Blind, stupid, America, . . . the one nation of the globe which has had offered to it the rich gifts that every people of Europe brought and laid at its feet, and it spurned them all."[10]

The Black, Red, and Brown Power movements of the 1960s and

1970s glorified the uniqueness of the races. Many white Americans began to search for something that did not make them appear to be "Anglo-bland, tasteless, and inert," something that gave them distinction and identity. Yet at the same time that Americans researched their roots, they also yearned to be part of a community. Deep down, many were reacting to what they considered a perpetually moving, individualistic society. They felt rootless. Some had a need to know that their history extended past their parents, past the impersonal, fragmented, solitary aspects of American society. They had to find a group to identify with, something deeper than an alumni association or a bowling league.[11]

For many, the solution that fulfilled both the need for a unique identity and the simultaneous desire to be a part of a community was to return to the ethnicity of their ancestors. However, the ethnicity they returned to took a new form, becoming a "symbolic ethnicity" that offered individuals the opportunity to select the most appealing aspects of the immigrant culture—the music, the dancing, the food—without suffering the ostracism of the stranger, the constant obstacles of the language barrier, or the loneliness endured by their immigrant ancestors. It was a period of searching for roots and forming new ethnic identities, valuable possessions at a time when much of America was struggling for identity. This "symbolic ethnicity" would provide the best of both worlds.[12]

For Basques in Idaho, it meant the full blooming of something that had been slowly growing over the decades. By this stage of assimilation, American Basques were now sufficiently established as Americans to look back to their heritage. It became apparent that this generation was to answer the inverse of the question asked by their parents and grandparents. Instead of "To what extent will I take on the ways of America?" the question now became "To what degree do I take on the ways of Basque culture?" Their Basque ethnicity provided opportunity for membership in a strong community, which had managed to set itself apart without alienating other Americans. The third generation had the convenience of a much wider, less threatening range of choices than their predecessors had. While some chose not to be involved in the Basque community at all, others made Basque culture an integral part of their lives. Some were so drawn that they moved back to the Basque Country. In general, Basques of the third generation, building on the foundation laid by the first and second generations, created something of a renaissance, a strong attraction toward involvement in elements of their culture and the study of their roots.

A large number of organizations sprouted to allow Basques to participate in this cultural resurgence. Besides the Oinkaris, dozens of organizations, clubs, and institutions came into being after 1960: in 1972 Anaia Danok (Brothers All), the first organization with a political orientation; in 1973 the North American Basque Organization (NABO), a federation of Basque centers throughout the United States; in 1974 a Boise State University year-long program set in the Basque Country; in the early 1980s Aiztan Artean, a Basque women's organization; in 1986 the Biotzetik Basque Choir; and, dedicated in 1987, the Basque Museum and Cultural Center in Boise.

The smorgasbord of choices for Basques in Idaho indicated the existence of a strong subculture throughout the twentieth century; there was a venue for practically every taste in politics, music, dancing, sports, history, language, and food. American Basques could simultaneously select elements of Basque culture that they enjoyed and maintain the conveniences of modern American living. The things that American Basques chose over the latter decades of the twentieth century were what would determine the changing makeup of the subculture.

Ethnic Studies

The study of historical and linguistic roots was not a priority for Basque immigrants, but it would become important to their children and grandchildren. Members of the Oinkari Basque Dancers, when traveling to perform in Idaho and other western states, would often be asked questions about the Basque Country. Many were embarrassed at their inability to speak the Basque language, and they began to feel that it was important to have at least a working knowledge of Euskera. In 1963 several approached Joe Eiguren about the possibility of his offering regular instruction. Even though he had no teaching experience, he accepted their proposal and organized the first Basque language class ever taught in Idaho and possibly in the United States. More than fifty students showed up for the first session. The *Idaho Statesman* reported: "Girls in ratted hairdos and boys in tennis shoes Tuesday night began the study of one of the world's most ancient languages." Joe Eiguren began slowly, at first concentrating solely on the alphabet and pronun-ciation, gradually moving to the most basic principles of Euskera's com-plicated grammar. The weekly classes, which were attended mostly by teenagers, with a sprinkling of adults, continued for two years. "Students realized how difficult the language really was," one observer noted.[13]

To accompany his classes, Eiguren published a fifty-page booklet, *The History and Origin of the Basque Language,* and in 1968 he com-pleted a Basque grammar and vocabulary book, *Euzkera Izketan Zelan Ikasi* (How to Learn to Speak Basque), which included thirty introduc-tory lessons on record albums to help beginners with pronunciation. In 1972 he published *The Basque History—Past and Present.* Eiguren was one of a few immigrants to work in this field, and his efforts at teaching Basque language and history were pioneering, among the first academic and cultural ventures undertaken in the United States.[14]

Besides his own efforts, Eiguren participated in the formation of a program that, though short-lived, created offshoots that spurred cul-tural studies through the end of the century. Throughout the nation in the 1960s and 1970s, studies of ethnic history became a magnet for funding from large foundations and public agencies. The notion of study of cultural roots was so popular that Congress passed the Ethnic Heritage Studies Program Act in the early 1970s to subsidize such en-deavors. A small group in the Basque community realized the potential for such study in Idaho, and the Idaho Division of Continuing Educa-tion wrote a grant proposal to the National Endowment for the Hu-manities calling for college courses in Basque culture, a Basque studies library, and a six-week program of travel in Euskadi for members of the Idaho Basque community. In the fall of 1971 the National Endowment for the Humanities awarded a two-year $52,285 grant, allowing Idaho to sponsor the Idaho Basque Studies Program. Years later, one of the grant writers commented, "It was the best grant project I've ever seen. More things came out of it. . . . We really got our money's worth."[15]

The Basque Studies Program formed a five-member advisory board to oversee direction of the grant. The board hired an executive secretary and held informational meetings in area towns to explain the program. The purpose of this endeavor, they said, was "to preserve and enhance the distinctive customs, traditions, and characteristics of the Basque culture in Idaho and surrounding states. It is a program about Basques, but it is a program for all people, Basque and non-Basque." The program proposed to accomplish this objective by "strengthening cultural pride and preserving cultural characteristics which lend variety and richness to our diverse American society."[16]

Encouraged by the program, Idaho's colleges and universities began to include Basque courses in their schedules. Boise State College offered two noncredit classes in Basque language, and courses in Basque culture were available at the University of Idaho and Idaho State University through the divisions of continuing education. The College of Southern Idaho also offered a Basque anthropology class. The program was praised as a "boost for the resurrection of ethnic roots." Besides its academic courses, the Basque Studies Program also began to organize Basque cultural and athletic events. Several board members formed a Basque choir, and plans were made for Basque instructors to travel to Idaho to teach young children traditional Basque musical instruments and dance steps. Another project that the program funded was the renovation of the indoor handball court at Anduiza's old boardinghouse on Grove Street in Boise, which had not been used for thirty years. Refuting earlier predictions about these courts, a group of volunteers painted the court's lines and repaired the roof, and the studies program organized regular *pala* and handball tournaments.[17]

By far the most visible event that the Basque Studies Program sponsored was a three-day festival in the summer of 1972. A precursor to the later Jaialdi festivals, the Holiday Basque Festival was described by an Idaho newspaper as "one of the largest celebrations of its kind ever held other than on Basque soil." The festival drew about five thousand people to Boise's Western Idaho Fairgrounds. The participants were treated to Basque weight-lifting and wood-chopping contests, singing and dancing performances, and sheepdog demonstrations. The festival site included historical-information booths, a sidewalk café, and a Basque art display. A *pala* tournament was held in the newly renovated handball court, won by two players from the French-Basque region of Lapurdi.[18]

Through the momentum of successes such as the 1972 festival, the Basque Studies Program continued to undertake projects well after its planned two-year life-span. Oral histories of Basque immigrants were recorded. The advisory board produced a short television documentary on the history of Basques in the state. In 1974 they sponsored Jon

Oñatibia, an instructor from the Basque Country, to travel to Idaho to teach language, music, and dance to young Basques. Though Jon Oñatibia stayed only briefly, he was adept at teaching words and music that remained in his students' minds long after his departure. Almost twenty years after taking his class, one of his students still recalled the lines from an Oñatibia song she had learned at age four: "Zu mutila al zara? Ez! Ez! Ez!" [Are you a boy? No! No! No!].[19]

*Second-generation Basque pala players at the Anduiza fronton in Boise, 1930s.
In the 1940s one sociologist predicted that the handball courts would "probably
remain as ruins when the last foreign-born pelota player has passed away."
Courtesy Basque Museum, Boise, Idaho.*

*Pete Cenarrusa, like many second-
generation Basques, served with the
United States military during
World War II. Cenarrusa later
became Speaker of the House,
secretary of state, and one of the
strongest American supporters of
Basque political causes. Courtesy
Basque Museum, Boise, Idaho.*

The Basque Company of the Ada County Volunteers, about half of whom were foreign-born, never saw any action during World War II. Still, they earned the respect of the local newspaper, which called them "a hard-hitting outfit of riflemen." Courtesy Basque Museum, Boise, Idaho.

Singers perform during a set change of the Song of the Basques, *1949. The production symbolized the renaissance that Basque-Americans would experience in the latter decades of the century. It was "the greatest night in the Basques' history in America," one reporter said. Courtesy Basque Museum, Boise, Idaho.*

Children pose with their teacher, Jay Hormaechea, before a performance, 1950. Many credit Hormaechea's dance lessons as the reason Basque culture continued to be practiced for the rest of the century. Courtesy Basque Museum, Boise, Idaho.

Boise's Basque Center opened in 1949 at a time when many nearby boarding-houses were closing. The Center, with its bar, kitchen, and dance hall, remained the social center of Boise's Basque community through the end of the century, hosting hundreds of Basque dances, wedding receptions, performances, rehearsals, and card tournaments. Courtesy Basque Museum, Boise, Idaho.

Beni Goitiandia lifts a 250-pound cylinder during a competition, 1961. Although few Basque-Americans participated in weight-lifting events, it was a reminder of their agrarian past and the kind of physical labor that immigrants hoped their children would not have to perform. Courtesy Basque Museum, Boise, Idaho.

Basque men watch Jose Luis Arrieta pull a 1,550-pound block during a competition at a Boise Basque picnic, 1975. Courtesy Basque Museum, Boise, Idaho.

The Oinkari dancers pose with Idaho politicians during their visit to Washington, D.C., 1964. Senator Frank Church (fifth from the left in light suit) was a long-time supporter of the Basques in his decades in Congress. During a 1978 visit to the Basque Country, he viewed the first legal display of the Basque flag since Franco assumed power in the 1930s. Courtesy Basque Museum, Boise, Idaho.

*Domingo Ansotegui (left)
and Jimmy Jausoro played
together for the Oinkari
dancers from the group's
beginning in 1960 until
Domingo's death in 1984.
In 1985 Jimmy received a
National Heritage Fellow-
ship in Washington, D.C.,
and continued to play at
dances more than sixty years
after his first gig. Courtesy
Basque Museum, Boise,
Idaho.*

*Joe Eiguren began teaching Basque-language classes in 1963, the first formal
attempt to revive the ancient language among American-born Basques. Although
few students became fluent, a small minority of Basques continued to preserve
the language through adult courses and a Basque preschool. Courtesy Basque
Museum, Boise, Idaho.*

The Anduiza fronton, built in 1915, was renovated in the early 1970s with financial help from the Basque Studies Program. A small but dedicated group of Basque Americans continued to play pala in the fronton through the 1990s. Courtesy Basque Museum, Boise, Idaho.

J. R. Simplot (left), the king of Idaho's potato industry, with Basque Country President Jose Antonio Ardanza during the president's visit to Idaho, 1988. Courtesy Basque Museum, Boise, Idaho.

More than 150 children came to weekly dance lessons at the Basque Center in Boise through the 1990s. "It's like parents are grasping for something," one Basque woman said. "They want their kids to have it. They don't want them to lose it." But some wondered if these children would find it worth the time to teach the dances when they became parents. Courtesy Basque Museum, Boise, Idaho.

10

The Modern Basque Country

The Studies Abroad Programs

Before the 1970s there were few opportunities for young Basque Americans to travel to Euskadi, fewer still to study the language and history of their antecedents. Some might have ventured there with their parents, visiting the family farm, struggling to snag words from the galloping table conversation of their relatives. Others, like the group who later formed the Oinkaris, saved for months and went on their own. These were generally brief sight-seeing trips, however, from which they would bring back wonderful slides and fond memories of the luscious cuisine, but only a sprinkling of new Basque words and a vague understanding of Basque history.

This situation would change after the 1972 summer study program in the Basque Country, sponsored by Idaho's Basque Studies Program. A small group involved with the program traveled for six weeks, spending half the time in the French-Basque town of Ustaritz, the other half in the Gipuzkoan mountain village of Arantzazu. For most, it was their first trip to the Basque Country, and it offered an opportunity for real immersion in Basque language, history, and culture. The experience compelled several in the group, upon their return to the United States, to do what they could to make it possible for others to have similar experiences.[1]

One member of the group, Pat Bieter, a professor at Boise State University, persuaded the school to establish a program in the Basque Country. "As I realized how much I learned and grew to appreciate and love the Basque Country on this trip," he said, "it dawned on me that we needed to get others from Idaho over there to meet family and learn more about the history and culture." Following up on contacts made during the 1972 trip, he established the program in the small Gipuzkoan town of Oñati, where a minicampus was established in a nearly vacant seminary. In the fall of 1974, seventy-five students and five faculty members became the first Americans to participate in an extended study program on Basque soil.[2]

Oñati was in many ways an ideal location. A town of about ten thousand, it had a high percentage of Basque speakers who used a dialect similar to that used by Basques in Idaho. The program offered various levels of Spanish and Basque language courses, Basque music and dancing lessons, Basque history, and Spanish literature. Trips through different regions of the Basque Country and Spain were organized. At night and on weekends, the students would venture into Oñati, meet Basque friends in the bars, and practice their Euskera or Spanish. For residents of the small town, it was odd to have so many Americans walking through their streets, conspicuously dressed in sweatshirts and blue jeans, many of the men with hair longer than most women had. Many were surprised that Americans would take such an interest in their traditions. "It made us curious," one Oñati resident said years later. "We had never met anybody that spoke Basque and not Spanish. It was very nice."[3]

The Americans of Basque ancestry were also surprised to find the region much different from the image that had been conveyed to them. What they imagined and the reality of the Basque Country were "pretty far apart," one program instructor said later, and they passed through a period of "disillusion" similar in many ways to that of Basque immigrants who returned to Euskadi after decades in the United States. One Idahoan who studied in the program said the people he met in Euskadi "weren't as Basque as I thought they'd be. Part of that was my understanding of what it meant to be Basque." It was odd, he recalled, to hear American rock music, to see young Basques wearing UCLA T-shirts, and to watch Festus from the American television classic *Gunsmoke* squawking in dubbed Spanish. "It seemed so funny. Here I was, trying to learn about my past and be more like them, and they were trying to be more like Americans."[4]

Some realized that their Basqueness in America was a different version of the culture they observed in the Basque Country. One student said of his experience, "When I got to the Basque Country, I realized I was different from what they were. Ironically, for the first time I realized I was an American—of Basque ancestry. It wasn't until I was outside the U.S. that I recognized this. Over time I also came to understand that what had developed in America was its own subculture, distinct from what was going on in Euskadi. I have to admit there was some identity crisis as I tried to sort all this out."[5]

Gradually many began to unearth new discoveries about the Basque culture, about what had survived and what had changed since the time when their grandparents emigrated. The program "changed them and what it meant for them to be Basque," Pat Bieter said. Months of living the Basque culture shaped them. They saw new Basque dances and new Basque celebrations, made new Basque friends, learned to speak Basque. Some even met their future spouses in the Basque Country. And though they represented a small portion of all Basque descendants in the state, participants in the year-long program returned with an interest for life in the Basque culture. "It changed me completely," said one student, a third-generation Basque who studied in Oñati from 1977 to 1978. "To know who you are and where you come from is important in directing where you're going in the future." The Boise State program, he said, was the catalyst for his heavy involvement in Basque culture. He returned to the Basque Country seven times over the next fifteen years, enrolled in the University of Nevada, Reno's Basque Studies Program, and became president of the North American Basque Association.[6]

"The program filled a profound need," said another third-generation Basque who attended the Oñati program. "There was definitely a need for people to find out about their roots, and the best way to find out about your roots is to go back to the original land." He studied in Oñati from 1978 to 1979 and made several extended trips over the next decade. "I have become much more active" in Idaho's Basque community, he said. "A good part of that is because of my trip."[7]

The Oñati program continued until 1980, after which Boise State, the University of Nevada, Reno, and several other schools formed a consortium program in Donosti/San Sebastián. The consortium offered many of the same courses as the Oñati program. The Basque Country programs, as one Idahoan said, "put a real shot of cultural adrenaline" into the state's Basque community. It gave the participating students the academic opportunities and background in Basque Country culture that earlier Basque Americans never had. Though relatively few attended the programs, they returned to have a strong impact on preserving the Basque subculture in Idaho. They pushed for authenticity and a revival of the Old Country ways in a manner never previously emphasized, affecting even those who would never have the opportunity to make their own treks to the Basque Country.[8]

A New Basque Nationalism

Americans traveling to the Basque Country in the 1960s and 1970s were often shocked by what they recognized to be the results of Civil War and decades of political and social oppression. Francisco Franco's attempts at erasing Basque culture in the years after the Spanish Civil War were immensely destructive, especially in Bizkaia and Gipuzkoa. Use of the Basque language was prohibited, and the generation of Basques who grew up in the postwar years remembered receiving slaps in the face or worse punishments for using the language in school. Later in life, people of this generation would be unable to recall much more than a handful of Basque words. Franco's efforts to eradicate the language were at least partially successful.[9]

Basques were also punished economically for their opposition to Franco. Spain as a whole was still a poor country into the 1950s; with its industrial tradition, however, the Basque region represented one of the few bright spots, making Franco even more determined to keep the Basques tied to the central Spanish economy. Heavy industry continued to flourish in Bizkaia and Gipuzkoa throughout the almost forty years of Franco's dictatorship. By 1970 the Basque regions, representing only 7 percent of Spain's population, controlled 17 percent of its bank assets and 33 percent of its shipyards and shipping lines. About half of the Basque workforce was employed in heavy industry. For most of the dictatorship, the Basque Country had the highest per capita income of Spain's fourteen economic regions, with Gipuzkoa, Bizkaia, and Araba at times ranked first, second, or third among all regions.[10]

The Franco dictatorship capitalized on this wealth. The four Basque regions contributed 13 percent of Spain's taxes. By 1971 Madrid took 30 billion pesetas in taxes from the Basque Country and returned 8.5 billion, less than one-third of the revenue contributed. During the 1960s, while tourism was becoming dominant in the rest of "sunny Spain," lit-

tle concern was given to the pollution dumping into the Basque regions. For Franco, the Basque Country became a messy industrial room
that Spain did not have to show to guests. Pollution spewed out of factories, powdering the sides of old buildings with dust and turning the
rivers industrial colors. There was still beauty in the Basque Country,
but more and more of that beauty was covered in grime.[11]

Hard times, however, proved to be galvanizing. As one historian suggested, in trying to destroy Basque culture and identity, "Spain had
been its own worst enemy." Basque nationalist sentiment flourished
during the four decades of Franco's rule. It began in underground associations formed in prisons after the Spanish Civil War and with Basque
mountain-climbing associations, small groups that met in isolated areas
to discuss preservation of their disappearing Basque identity. In 1947
exiles established Radio Euzkadi to broadcast news and nationalist
propaganda to the Basque Country. Later, strikes and demonstrations
proved that Franco's suppression made Basques only more aggressive,
more conscious of what might be lost.[12]

Although Basque nationalists from the time of Sabino Arana had insisted on a nonviolent movement, by the 1960s a militant branch of
Basque revolutionaries formed ETA, an acronym for Euskadi ta Askata-
suna (Basque Country and Freedom). ETA's roots were at Bilbao's University of Deusto, a Jesuit institution where seven students first met in
1952 to discuss Basque nationalism. The group grew, seeking to preserve
the Basque language and culture through clandestine distribution of
publications. Other organizations splintered off throughout the Basque
region, concentrating on various projects, such as forming dance troupes
and volunteering in secret Basque language schools. Throughout the
1950s an element of these student groups became increasingly nationalist. ETA originally concentrated on propaganda and cultural preservation, but a wing of the group began to discuss the need for armed re-
taliation against Franco's suppression. In 1961 ETA undertook its first
act of sabotage, planting a bomb to derail a train carrying hundreds of
Franco supporters to a rally. Although the weak explosion failed to derail the train, one hundred ETA members were arrested and tortured.
The incident propelled many members of ETA to embrace violence as
the most effective means to achieve independence. In 1962 several of
the group's founders issued a statement proclaiming ETA to be "a clandestine revolutionary organization with three fronts: cultural, political

and military." The first ETA-related death was actually the killing of one of its own members by Spanish Civil Guards in 1968, initiating a cycle of violence that took hundreds of lives over the next decades. In tune with social upheaval around the world in the 1960s and 1970s, hundreds of thousands of young Basques marched in the streets demanding independence from Spain, often setting off explosive counterattacks by Spanish police, who attempted to shut them down with rubber bullets and tear gas. The turbulence of the period rubbed off on Basque Americans, creating one of the first instances of their political involvement.[13]

An Active Exception

"Nationalism is only a shadow here in the largest Basque settlement in the United States," a *New York Times* reporter wrote of Idaho's Basque community in 1970. Even though there were "dissent, demonstrations and strikes" in the Basque Country, he added, "at the Sheepherders' Ball [in Boise] there were no patriotic speeches, no moments of silent prayer, no ringing declarations, not even looks of grave concern at the plight of the people in Spain." As their reaction to the Spanish Civil War had demonstrated, Basque immigrants in Idaho generally hesitated to plunge into the political and societal problems of their native land. Many had sidestepped the nationalist furor and the pervasive persecution during the Franco era. The generation of Basques immigrating after the 1950s, however, experienced the turmoil, and some were themselves political exiles. After arriving in Idaho, they often found a small but rapt audience of politically aware members of the Basque community, most notably Idaho's Basque secretary of state, Pete Cenarrusa. Their experiences led to a brief period of political involvement by Idaho's Basque community during the last gasping years of the Franco dictatorship in the 1970s. The period, however, marked an activist exception that proved the prevailing hands-off rule.[14]

Some of the first activity was sparked in late 1970, when sixteen Basque men and women were tried in the city of Burgos for the murder of a Spanish police commissioner. The Burgos 16, all of whom admitted to being members of ETA, were subjected to a summary court-martial in which they barely had access to their attorneys. The trial was clearly a show of power by Franco's regime, because, as historian Robert P. Clark wrote, "The Burgos court regarded the sixteen accused ETA members not as the true authors of the crime, but rather as the symbols of revolutionary Basque separatism." Although the evidence against the defendants was questionable, all sixteen were found guilty and six were sentenced to death before a firing squad. The Burgos trial attracted international attention, with governments around the globe demanding that the Franco government commute the death sentences.[15]

The Basque community in Idaho adamantly protested. Secretary of State Pete Cenarrusa was one of the leaders in this effort. Born to immigrant parents, Cenarrusa first learned of the poor treatment of Basques during the Spanish Civil War and hoped to help the cause one day. After being elected to the legislature, and later appointed as secretary of state, Cenarrusa was in a position to do so. He persuaded Idaho governor Don Samuelson to send a cable to General Franco requesting that the case be transferred from a military to a civil court. Next, he convinced Idaho's congressional delegation to ensure that "immediate action" be taken through the State Department to pressure the Spanish government.

The day after the death sentences were handed down, more than two hundred Basque Americans met at the Boise Basque Center to draft a telegram to Franco: "200 representatives of over 12,000 Basque people [in Idaho] request, your excellency, that clemency be handed with respect to the [death sentences] by the military tribunal." Tension built until finally, on December 30, 1970, one day before three prisoners were to be executed by firing squad, Franco commuted the death sentences of the six Basques to thirty years in prison. A moment of silence was observed in thanksgiving at a Burgos benefit dance in the Basque Center in Boise.[16]

After the conflict, Pete Cenarrusa visited the Basque Country for the first time. Following emotional visits with his parents' families, he met with the Basque government in exile and ETA members hiding in the French side of the Basque Country. This experience further convinced him that he should help in whatever way he could, and when he returned he joined a group called Anaia Danok (Brothers All). This organization, according to one of its founding members, "wanted to educate the people of Idaho, Basque and non-Basque, about what was going on politically in the Basque Country." Besides the reaction to the trial at Burgos, Anaia Danok became the first organization in Idaho with any connection to politics in Euskadi. Anaia Danok attracted about fifty members, both Basque and non-Basque, with heavy involvement by more recent immigrants and American-born Basques who had traveled to the Basque Country. The group met once a month and sponsored dinners, lectures, and an oral history collection of early Basque immigrants in the state.[17]

Cenarrusa worked hard to draft a document dedicated to calling attention to the Basque situation. He hoped that a strongly worded statement passed by a bipartisan American state legislature would succeed in drawing national attention to the cause. The result was that Idaho, "one of the most conservative states in the Union, passed a declaration of solidarity with insurrectionists against a Cold War ally, whose support through leases of land for air and naval bases had been considered essential to the protection of Europe and the Mediterranean." The fact that this resolution passed demonstrated the respect that Basques had earned, and the initiative of Pete Cenarrusa in particular. The document spread in Basque spheres throughout the world and was recognized by the exiled Basque leader, President Jesús María Leizaola.[18]

Cenarrusa continued to work with international Basque nationalists, and Anaia Danok took one of its strongest stands in 1975 after two Basque separatists convicted of killing Spanish police were executed by firing squad. The executions aroused protests throughout Western Europe, and at least sixteen nations recalled their ambassadors. When the United States government did not formally protest, Anaia Danok began a lobbying effort to compel the government to sever diplomatic relations with Franco and to seek Spain's expulsion from the United Nations. The United States government "hasn't done anything for our people against the Franco government," one member of Anaia Danok said at the time. "The American government is supposed to protect liberty and democracy, but instead we have helped a dictator like Franco." Another member called U.S. policy toward Spain "one of the great hypocrisies of American foreign policy."[19]

A week after the executions, 150 Basques gathered for a mass at St. John's Cathedral in Boise. The service, held in Basque and English, offered prayers "for our Basque brothers and sisters and for conversion of our enemies." Speakers during the mass encouraged Basques in Idaho to "do all we can to bring about an end of suffering and inhumanity in Spain." Several days later two members of Anaia Danok flew to Washington, D.C., to meet with Idaho's congressional delegation. They sought support for a resolution to cut off U.S. aid and to sever diplomatic ties with Spain. Although none of the House or Senate members agreed to sponsor the resolution, Senator Frank Church, then chairman of the Foreign Relations Committee, told the Anaia Danok representatives that he would work on pressuring the Franco government by cutting back on military aid.[20]

From the beginning of his political career Church had been a strong supporter of the Basques; his wife, Bethine Church, said he had always considered the Basques "a major part of the community." After entering office, she said, the senator "began to get all these letters and pleas, and he was really sensitized to the Basque question. He thought [Basques] were getting a raw deal. And they were." In the 1950s and 1960s, Church, along with other members of the delegation, sponsored legislation to help Basque sheepherders gain citizenship. He later used his position on the Senate Foreign Relations Committee to voice opposition to the Franco government. "I can see no justification for American dollars being sent to a Spanish government intent on persecuting the families of thousands of outstanding American citizens," he said in 1968. He had been vocal during the Burgos trial. Even after Franco died, he continued to push for Basque freedom. "Unfortunately, the Spanish government still falls short in guaranteeing the Basques full political and civil rights."[21]

In 1978 Church became the first U.S. senator to visit the Basque Country. "Frank felt so strongly about Idaho's Basque citizenry who had asked for help," Bethine Church said. "He really wanted to go." Invited by Basque leaders, Church flew to Bilbao for the first public celebration of Aberri Eguna (Day of the Homeland) since the 1930s. As their plane was about to land in Bilbao, Bethine Church recalled, the senator looked out the window at the large crowd gathered at the airport and said, "'There must be someone important coming in on this plane.' And I said, 'Yeah, it looks like it. There's certainly a big group of people out there.' And we got to the door—and they were all there for us!"[22]

The Churches walked off the plane under hoops held by dancers, shook hands with Basque dignitaries, and began a whirlwind tour to several Basque towns, including Gernika and Donosti. At one dinner in his honor Church told his hosts, "You can be proud of the people you have sent to our state. They are not only good, loyal Americans, but

Basques who have preserved their culture, their dances, their language, and who have done much to enrich the life of Idaho." On Sunday, March 26, he stood on a balcony in Bilbao to watch a parade in honor of Aberri Eguna, which featured the first legal display of the Basque flag since the beginning of the Franco dictatorship. Bethine Church recalled that thousands of people chanted, "Frank Church!" and waved in his direction. The senator at that point turned to the Basque dignitaries and commented, "You know, it's obvious to me that I'm running for election in the wrong country."[23]

It was clear that the political work of Basques in Idaho played a role in spurring support from Idaho's congressional delegation. Anaia Danok had other successes. The group sponsored its own celebration of Aberri Eguna in Boise, where the Basque flag was raised at the state capitol, and a mass and lunch were held at the Basque Center. Anaia Danok also began to raise money, which was funneled to a group from the French Basque regions that provided protection for political refugees. "We [Anaia Danok] are getting stronger," one member told the *Idaho Statesman* in 1975. "Many people won't let you use their name for fear of reprisal, but they will slip you a $20 bill."[24]

But this fear of reprisal, the deep-seated suspicion of Basque immigrants for things political, and disinterest by the larger portion of Basque Americans mostly ended the brief period of involvement by the Idaho Basque community. Pete Cenarrusa's office became a clearinghouse for such Basque problems as passports, visas, extensions, herders' tax problems, and citizenship issues, but those were local and individual concerns. Anaia Danok remained active through the 1970s but eventually disbanded. "People here did not understand the political struggle," one Anaia Danok member said years later. "This was a time when we could have united behind the Basque Country and really done some good. We never accomplished that goal." (Perhaps their efforts, coupled with the media attention that the Basque independence movement gained in the United States, did contribute to one sharp realization in the Basque-American community—a distinction between Basque and Spanish. Membership in Boise's Euzkaldunak Club had always been open to anyone with Basque or Spanish roots. In 1975 the club's bylaws were amended to allow only those of Basque heritage to become members.) The period marked a further divergence in the path of Idaho's Basque community from the Basque Country's course and again reflected the relevance of elements that would be chosen—or, perhaps more appropriately, *not* chosen.

Returning to the Old Country

When Basques who had spent thirty years or more in Idaho returned to native villages for good, the societal and political changes often bewildered them. Their return was sometimes a disappointment. They had worked, most of them for decades, to acquire enough savings to retire in Euskadi, and images of their glorious return had run through their heads for many years. They hoped to play the role of hometown hero who had made good in America, who had often sent back money to pay for his family's modern farm machinery or their apartment in town. For many, the experience in America had changed them. Friends and family who had remained behind all those years often felt that the Amerikanuak, as they called those who had immigrated, "suffered modifications in their personalities" and were unable to behave normally around people again. The Amerikanuak would sometimes find themselves relating only to others who had been in the American West, and they would gather at tables in bars or restaurants, talking about how life might have been better in Idaho.[25]

Even Basques who returned for short visits often suffered letdowns from their old country. Things would appear smaller to them than they remembered, dirtier, older, run-down. Even in the most remote villages they could see the influence of the movement of Spaniards into the region; more Spanish was spoken on the street, and there were more blue-collar neighborhoods in the cities. The Basque Country had also modernized, even in rural areas. In 1962 an Idaho newspaper reported what one Basque man had been surprised to see on his first return to Euskadi after thirty-one years in Idaho: When he had left the Basque Country in 1931, "the women wore the white blouses and cotton skirts associated with the Basques, not dresses ending at the knee. They wore their long braids coronet fashion, not bouffant hairdos. Their stockings were hand-knitted, thick and black, not seamless nylons. And when they cooked, it was over a wood stove, not on a gas range." The homes of their childhood now boasted televisions and stereos, and their beautiful village church was marred by graffiti.[26]

Sometimes the disappointment was directed at the returnee. The

Amerikanuak had not done as well as expected. "Everybody thinks you're going to be a millionaire," one Basque returnee said. "I barely had shoes on. After forty years of watching American movies, they think that everybody has a nice car and a swimming pool and a beautiful home." Although reunions with relatives and friends were generally happy occasions, there was often an awkward period of readjustment, especially for Basques who had not seen their homeland for up to sixty years. In 1952 one Basque immigrant to Idaho returned to his wife and four children—whom he had not seen in thirty-two years. His young-est boy, two years old when his father left for Idaho, was now thirty-four. (The father said at the time that despite the availability and con-venience of flying, he planned on returning to the Basque Country by boat. "Planes may be fine," he said, "but I'm not in that much of a hurry to go home. After being away for thirty-two years, a few days more or less are of no consequence.")[27]

Air travel made trips more accessible for Basque Americans. In the summer of 1971, 183 Basques returned on a charter organized by Euz-kaldunak. Joaquin Arte was returning for the first time in sixty-two years. One woman, making her first trip to the Basque Country after forty-nine years in Idaho, saw her brother for the first time.[28] Travelers were often surprised at what they saw in Euskadi. In 1970 Harmon Travel Service of Boise organized what it called "the Basque Olé Tour." An *Idaho Statesman* reporter who joined the group of twenty Basques on the tour noted the "disturbing" signs of political unrest that the group saw as it visited the coastal city of Donosti. One protest by a Basque man at a handball court was especially disconcerting: "He lit a match to his gasoline-soaked clothes and jumped into the pelota court in front of Generalissimo Franco, shouting 'Gora Euskadi!'"

Sometimes, after the initial awkwardness subsided, the visits to their homeland would cause Basque immigrants to question their decision to move to the United States. Their families had experienced a different life, the friends they knew had survived the toughest years of the war, and some had even become wealthy. Since he had left, one Basque im-migrant said, "things changed 1,000 percent, and the people that stayed over there . . . are better off today than we are." His friends had apart-ments on the coast, enjoyed month-long vacations in Italy. Some Basques in Idaho felt that emigrating had been a mistake, that their de-cision to leave had been an abandonment of their roots. "Forty years later," one Basque man said of his emigration, "you realize that what you gave up is more than what you gained [in Idaho]. For a few dollars, you sold your soul, you sold your family, you lose everything. . . . Forty years later, I'm still a foreigner, an immigrant. You give a lot more than you gained."[29]

Another Basque immigrant said that despite his financial successes in the United States, "I also missed out on a few things along the way." He remembered that the first thousand dollars he was able to save from his first year of herding was sent in the form of a cashier's check to his father back home. "He never got it. He had died. He was in the hospital when I sent it. I didn't have the money to go to his funeral because I had already sent everything to him a month earlier."[30]

But most seemed glad to return to Idaho. One Basque woman said her visit to the Basque Country was "like a lovely dream. . . . But I like to get back to the United States. This is my own country now and it is better." They had new families and friendships in Idaho, and they had grown accustomed to the dry weather, the household amenities, the political freedom. In Idaho the Basque dancers could perform with the *ikurrina,* the Basque flag; in Euskadi, during the Franco years, the Basque flag was prohibited. In Idaho the children and grandchildren of Basque immigrants were following the customs they had grown up with in Bizkaia, but young people in the Basque Country were changing. They sometimes felt that Idaho offered a newer, more ideal kind of Basque community. As one Basque man said in the 1960s after returning from a visit to his hometown in Bizkaia, "We do more of the traditional Basque dances in Boise than they do in Ispaster."[31]

11

The End of an Era

Backed by decades of influence in Idaho's sheep industry and demonstrated dramatically by the rationale behind the Sheepherders' Laws, young Basque men were still prized as employees into the 1970s and 1980s. Later immigrants benefited from Basques' established reputation and the easier travel. "I drank cognac my first night in the States," recalled one herder who immigrated in the late 1960s. "We came over in a big group and met Basques along the way. [The trip] was all taken care of for us, and it only took one day. Lots of people from the area I grew up in had been here, and I knew what things were going to be like. Herders who came earlier in the century," he said, "had a harder time than we did. It was much easier for us that came later."[1]

As in earlier days, there were recruiters in Bizkaia to find young men willing to enter into the three-year contracts established as a result of the earlier Sheepherders' Laws. The new sheepherders came on temporary three-year work visas, but they often renewed their contracts, and many chose to stay permanently. Through the early 1960s, these contracts still offered an attractive opportunity to a young man in rural Bizkaia. They could earn three or four times more than from a wage job back home, and the isolated sheepherding life, though improved from earlier times, still encouraged them to save their money.

As had always been the case, few had sheepherding experience, but the nature of their contract labor required them to show that they were up to the task, to prove, as one Basque contractor described it, "that you're not going to take over some office job from an American." One herder later claimed that officials even checked contractors' hands to attest to sheepherding skills. Even though he had worked on a farm his whole life, he spent days roughing up his hands to form calluses. "'This has got to be one hard-working guy,'" he claimed his inspector said. "'Look at those hands!'"[2]

Later herders, often as frugal as their predecessors, would make enough from their three-year contracts to remain successful for the rest of their lives. Although perhaps a bit more familiar with the United States through movies and the exaggerated stories of herders who returned to the Basque Country, they were still impressed by America. "Beautiful buildings! Clean streets!" a Bizkaian recalled of his first impression upon coming to Idaho in the 1960s. "I loved the cars over here. I didn't even own a bicycle in the Basque Country. I thought, 'You put me in one of those cars, and I'll faint.'" Many did fulfill their dreams of wealth. One man who immigrated "with seven bucks" had saved enough after four years to buy a condominium in the Bizkaian town of Gernika. They often used their savings to invest in new businesses or complete their education, marrying and settling in Idaho. They remained grateful for the opportunity that immigrating had made for them. "[The United States] made me what I am," one herder remarked. "I've never been unemployed here. Plenty of food on the table. This country has helped me a lot. And it still has opportunities. This is the best country in the world, I think."[3]

In the past these kinds of attitudes had helped keep a steady stream of young Basques interested in moving to the United States. By the 1970s, however, Basque immigration into Idaho had slowed drastically. The sheep industry, which had been the bridge for Basques to Idaho all along, was on a downward trend. Synthetic materials were replacing wool in clothing produced in the country, and the industry was not as profitable as it had once been. Reflecting a nationwide slowdown, sheep outfits in Idaho began to shut down in response to the decreased demand and the reduced availability of grazing land. In 1940 almost 1.4 million head of sheep grazed in Idaho; in 1970 there were only 773,000, and by the mid-1990s fewer than 250,000.[4]

Back in Euskadi the success stories of Basques who immigrated to America began to seem like relics of the past. They were replaced by accounts refuting the benefits of sheepherding. In their seminal work

Amerikanuak, William A. Douglass and Jon Bilbao wrote that a Basque priest, Father Santos Recalde, upon returning to Euskadi after a brief assignment ministering to Basques in Idaho, attacked the treatment of sheepherders in the American West in several prominent Spanish newspapers. He described sheepherding as "inhumane and exploitative." Father Recalde even tried to organize a labor union among contract herders. A newsletter, "El Pastor" (The Herder), served to spread word of their mistreatment. His efforts, however, were unsuccessful, and only a few of the herders joined the union. Other newspapers in the Basque Country carried stories about the misery of herding. In 1971 one newspaper based there ran a series of articles on the plight of herders in the American West; one headline reported, ONLY ONE OF EVERY HUNDRED BASQUE HERDERS IN THE UNITED STATES MAKES HIS FORTUNE.[5]

Perhaps most significant, the improvement in the economy of the Basque Country and all of Spain after the 1960s made immigrating unnecessary and unattractive. Spain, isolated for the decades following the Civil War, was slowly beginning to catch up with other Western European countries. Wages in the Basque Country climbed—at the same time herders' pay in Idaho was stagnating. Basques could stay in their hometown and earn just as much as—and, in many cases, more than—they could earn herding sheep in the Idaho hills. There seemed to be little incentive to leave the Basque Country, especially after the death of Franco in 1975. Although the political situation in the Basque Country would remain unstable with the continued violence and the incessant squabbling among Basque nationalist parties, the lives of most Basques continued to improve markedly. By the 1980s the choice for young Basques of whether to stay in their hometowns or to emigrate became no choice at all.

This immigration slowdown was highly apparent in Idaho. There were fewer and fewer Basque sheepherders showing up in Idaho towns on seasonal breaks, and those who did usually had been in the state for decades and had turned into "lifers." Now in their fifties and sixties, many of these herders became fixtures in the towns of central and southern Idaho. In some cases they had endeared themselves to Idahoans, who viewed older Basque herders as lonely remnants of an Old West lifestyle. But they were the exceptions. Immigrants from Central and South America began to replace Basques in the shrinking pool of sheep industry employees. An *Idaho Statesman* headline in the late 1970s reflected the new trend: MEXICANS, PERUVIANS SUPPLANT IDAHO'S SHEEP-HERDING BASQUES.[6]

The Decline of Euskera

During the twentieth century the Basque language had become recognized as the most important aspect of Basque identity. Valuing Euskera as another barrier from Spaniards, Sabino Arana tied Basque language and separatism so tightly together that it became absolutely essential to preserve the mother tongue. "The difference in race is proved by the difference of languages," one Basque nationalist wrote in 1906. "The Basque language differs radically from all the rest of the languages. So the race differs from all the remaining races." In the absence of any strong genetic or physical characteristics to distinguish a Basque race, nationalists fell back on the one trait that truly set Basques apart.[7]

The push to preserve the language in Euskadi became even stronger as a result of the efforts by Franco's dictatorship to erase it from existence. In the 1950s Basques began to organize clandestine elementary schools called *ikastolak,* in which at least part of the children's education was in Euskera. After Franco's death, the number of *ikastolak* increased dramatically, and Basque language academies opened for adults who did not have the opportunity to learn the language during the years of the dictatorship. The Basque government spent billions of pesetas for Basque schools, Basque radio and television stations, and Basque publications. The linguistic revival took on almost moral implications as the attitude prevailed among many that if there was no Basque language, then there would be no more Basque identity. One popular Basque song asked, "Don't you know that Euskera is the thing that makes us Basque?"[8]

For the most part, however, Basques who immigrated to Idaho did not impart this idea to their children. Basque was the language most immigrants had spoken since childhood and the language most used at home, but they realized it was not useful for their children in the United States. Their children and grandchildren would be Americans, and they did not need Basque to separate them from anyone else. Linda Barrinaga recalled that shortly before she left to study Euskera for a year in the Basque Country, her Basque grandmother discouraged her. "She told me, 'Basque will get you nowhere; learn Spanish.'"[9]

Few American-born Basques took advantage of the Basque classes that were offered, and even fewer stuck with it past the point of simple conversation. "The reality is," William A. Douglass wrote, "that formal Basque language courses have little real attraction and even less staying power, whether initiated by concerned private parties or by institutions." Joe Eiguren began his Basque class in 1963 with more than fifty students; two years later all but a handful had dropped out and the course was canceled. "Students realized how difficult the language really was," one observer noted. Other formal courses at Boise State University have had low enrollments, and the overwhelming majority of students who travel to the Basque Country study Spanish.[10]

Many problems that plague the survival of the Basque language in Euskadi also work against its preservation in Idaho—the varying dialects, the bewildering grammar. The majority of Basques in Idaho have little access to learning materials or conversational partners. So while most Basque Americans realize the importance of the language to the culture, ultimately they have not deemed worthwhile the daunting task of studying the language of their ancestors.

For the most part, Euskera was a casualty as Basque Americans chose how they wanted to be Basque. As one sociologist wrote, descendants of immigrants "are free to sort through their cultural inheritance and select this or that trait to be used or developed as one displays ancestral linens, pots or glassware." Given the difficulty of learning Euskera and their constant exposure to English, Basque Americans usually determined that the price of learning Basque was too high and chose to adopt other, more accessible aspects of the culture. Many Basque Americans chose not to place the kind of importance on Euskera that Basques in Europe have. "I think the language is important," one third-generation Basque American said. "But one time I overheard somebody saying that if you didn't speak Basque, then you weren't Basque. I wanted to beat the living hell out of that guy."[11]

Yet another third-generation Basque said, "I would give my right leg to be able to talk to my kids every day in Basque. . . . I'm doing everything I can to see that the culture is passed on. But the one thing I still want them to have is the language.'"[12] A minority did take the time to learn, in some cases even attempting to raise their children speaking Basque. Euskera offered them a chance to return to their roots, and for some, an opportunity to do something unique. One Basque American who traveled to the Basque Country to learn Euskera said he earned the admiration of his American friends. "They say, 'Wow, you can speak Basque!' They think it's pretty cool."

Yet even those who chose the ideal of learning Euskera in the Basque Country often discovered there was not much of a practical application for their endeavor. Their textbook, *Batua* (unified Basque language dialect largely introduced by the Basque Language Academy in the late 1960s and 1970s), was not always useful when, upon their return to the United States, they tried to speak with Basque immigrants; it was much like a foreign student of Oxford English attempting to carry on a conversation with a rural Mississippian. One language student recalled that after he returned to Boise he was excited to practice his newly acquired Euskera on first-generation Basques. "I came back with the idea, 'Hey, I'm going to be able to speak to these guys a lot better.'" But he found he had "a tough time" understanding their dialect.[13]

Besides the few Basque Americans who made Herculean efforts, the majority of Basques in Idaho had neither the time nor the resources to push on with the task. Boise's Basque Museum and Cultural Center offered evening classes, but these were attended by only a small group of the faithful. Only a few staple Basque words, like *amuma* (grandmother), would land on the tongues of the third generation. The fading of Euskera from the Idaho Basque community offered one of the most obvious differences between the culture they had created and the one they had left behind.

Music and Dancing Survive

The Basque language may have been dying out, but there were plenty of other cultural, or subcultural, elements that were flourishing. Basque cuisine remained popular, especially during holidays and Basque celebrations. (One American-born Basque said, "My kids would just not enjoy Thanksgiving dinner unless they had my mother's codfish with red peppers.") Even though Basque restaurants were more prevalent in other Basque communities in the American West, especially in Nevada and California, several experienced some success in Idaho. In 1979 the Boarding House restaurant opened in downtown Boise. Later, in 1987, Jesus Alcelay, a Basque chef, opened the Oñati Basque Restaurant, named after his hometown, where many Basque Americans had studied in Boise State's program. The restaurants were popular among non-Basques, but the most famous item was the chorizo, the sausage that had become a staple of most hot-dog carts and at the annual Western Idaho Fair. Some Italian restaurants even offered a "Basque Special" pizza, smothered in chorizo and peppers.

The traditions that survived within the subculture of the Basque community in Idaho were frequently the ones that returned the greatest enjoyment for the least time commitment. The visual, unmistakable ties to the Basque culture, such as dancing and music, that, unlike Euskera, did not require years of painstaking study were good candidates for survival. The Oinkaris thrived, as one dancer suggested, because the group "is the most fun thing Basques have going for them in this valley." Oinkari performances were enjoyable and exciting for both participants and spectators. The Basque dances, open to the general public, could be enjoyed without knowledge of one step or one word of Basque, though it was fun for non-Basques to give both a try. But for Basque Americans who chose to participate in Basque music and dancing groups, the dances offered another opportunity to experience the best of both worlds. They could do something different from mainstream America and at the same time genuinely be part of a strong community rich in ethnic flavor.[14]

From the beginning, music and dancing provided the thread of continuity through the Basque experience in Idaho. "Even with all the disagreements between people," one Idaho Basque said, "when the music started and the dancing began, they came together. It is the single cultural trait that has lasted from the beginning, and it is still the basis for our culture that we have here today." The difference now, as the third generation grew up, was the development of more formalized opportunities. The early, informal dances at the boardinghouses, where boarders would shove tables and chairs aside to make room for dancing, were eventually replaced with organized dances attended by Basques of all ages.[15]

This was especially evident with the Oinkaris. The group kept growing after its early success, traveling to the Montreal World's Fair, performing in places as far away as Milwaukee and Washington, D.C. By the early 1970s, however, the group seemed to have reached a plateau. They had hardly expanded their repertoire since the 1964 trip to New York. "It seemed like it had lost direction," said one Oinkari. "We were

performing, but we weren't growing." The next decade, however, demonstrated the benefits that increased travel to the Basque Country would
have for Idaho's Basque community. Participants in the overseas program would watch performances in the Basque Country, which inspired
them to return with photographs, films, videos, and costumes, and teach
those who did not attend the program. "The program was the re-
grounding of everything," said Gina Urquidi, a longtime dance director. "Once the group of people that had been to the Basque Country
got to be leaders Oinkaris [of Oinkari] I think it just flourished. It gave
everybody a sense of direction."[16]

There was a new emphasis on authenticity and broadening the scope
of the repertoire. By the early 1980s the Oinkaris were performing
dances from each of the seven Basque regions, with more than a dozen
different costumes. With the help of some returnees and special per-
mission, dance director John Ysursa taught some of the Oinkari men
traditional religious dances from the town of Oñati, where the Boise
State campus had been, and incorporated them into Boise's annual San
Inazio Festival, dancing outside and on the altar of St. John's Cathedral
during mass.

The new enthusiasm culminated in a decision by the group to travel
to the Basque Country to mark its twenty-fifth anniversary in 1985. For
almost two years Oinkari members held fund-raisers to earn the more
than $100,000 needed for the trip. One of the biggest fund-raising
events was *Nundik Nora* (From Here to Where?), a play written by
several Oinkaris that told the story of Basque immigration to Idaho
through music and dance. In June sixty dancers and musicians departed
for the three-week tour, which took them throughout the Basque Country for a series of performances. Basques were often intrigued by the visiting Americans, who, as several remarked to members of the group at
the time, seemed more interested in Basque culture than many young
people in the Basque Country were. For most Oinkaris, it marked their
first trip to the Basque Country, their first encounters with relatives and
with the realities of post-Franco Euskadi.[17]

The 1985 trip, along with consistent visits by dancers to the Basque
Country and greater access to sheet music and videotapes, allowed the
Oinkaris to increase the quantity and authenticity of their repertoire.
The group "looks more refined, more professional, looks more ethnic,"
said Albert Erquiaga, an Oinkaris founder. The 1960 group had been

"Americanized," he added. "We didn't know any better." Most essentially, the group continued to play its role in bringing young Basque Americans into the "Basque fold," as one described. "Oinkaris is really the only thing that immersed me in the idea of an American-Basque culture. . . . It's the most valuable tool we have in this valley to help young American Basques from Boise grow up in the cultural way, the social way, in every way." The Oinkaris became a trademark for the Basque community in Idaho. Most tourism brochures featured a snapshot of the dancers, a colorful highlight of the unique Basque presence in the state.[18]

At the center of the Oinkaris' sustained success, as always, was the group's longtime accordionist, Jimmy Jausoro, and tambourine player Domingo Ansotegui. The two had been playing since the Oinkaris' first performance, and they became some of the most readily identified Basques in the West. (When Ansotegui died in 1984, the Oinkaris danced the Oñati religious dances at his funeral, a tribute to his importance to the Idaho Basque community.) Jausoro kept playing for the Oinkaris and for the children's dancing group, accompanied by a new tambourine player, Juan Zulaika. In 1985 Jausoro traveled to Washington, D.C., to receive the National Heritage Fellowship. In tribute, Steve Siporin of the Idaho Commission on the Arts said, "Jimmy exemplifies the way in which an artistic tradition, personified and carried forward by an individual folk artist, can become the dynamic expression that binds an ethnic community together."[19]

His desire to continue playing demonstrated the importance that individual choice would have in maintaining the Basque subculture in Idaho. After six decades of playing at dances, nearly fifty years of playing for children's jota lessons, and more than thirty years of playing for the Oinkaris, Jimmy was frequently asked if he thought about quitting. "Well, yeah, I guess I should," he said. "But I enjoy it. If I didn't, I wouldn't be doing it. I just hang in there and play. And as long as they want me to play, why, I'll try to do the job."[20]

The Oinkaris were not the only Basque cultural institution that would thrive. An increasing number of formal organizations came into being that did not require a great investment of time yet offered Basque Americans an enjoyable way to maintain a communal tie. Singing had always been an important part of Basque celebrations, from the time when boarders would belt out songs at the dinner table to player pianos, guitars, accordions, and tambourines. But it was not until the early 1970s that a Basque choir formed in Boise. The group performed as part of the 1972 summer festival in Boise and later disbanded, but in 1986 several members of the Basque community decided to regroup for the first Jaialdi International Basque Festival. The choir, Biotzetik (From the Heart), continued to sing even after the event, and began performing at Basque festivals and weddings and at the annual Basque singing competition in Gardnerville, Nevada. Unlike the Oinkaris, Biotzetik opened its membership to non-Basques.

The Basque dances continued to thrive through the 1990s and were popular among non-Basques. Although the music of Jimmy Jausoro's orchestra was still popular, part of the reason the dances flourished was the formation of the rock-and-roll band Ordago in 1986. Ordago (meaning "there it is," a term from the card game *mus*) was the idea of several Oinkaris. After holding informal jam sessions for several months, Ordago's members asked Jimmy Jausoro if they could play during a set break at the Sheepherders' Ball in Emmett. Ordago's debut, according to Ron Lemmon, a founding member, was humble. "We did five songs and two of them twice." But the group practiced more and expanded its repertoire, then played to a crowd of thousands at the 1987 Jaialdi Festival. After that, Ordago began to get private gigs, especially at Basque festivals and weddings throughout the West. The group's unique blend of music, mixing classic American and Basque rock 'n' roll, jazzed up versions of traditional Basque songs. Their third set for a 1991 Ontario, Oregon, Basque dance was typical: "Pretty Woman," "Good Lovin'," "Euskotarrak," "Jota/Porrusalda," "Telebista," "Twist and Shout," "So Lonely," "Johnny B. Goode," "Bakarrik Lo Ez," "Stand by Me," and "Rock eta Rollin."[21]

The development of Ordago proved that the Basque-American subculture needed to adapt in order to survive. "We are what [Jimmy Jausoro's band] was forty years ago," one member said. "Our music is popular because we play for the people who end up dancing the most—the young people." The group even wrote its own songs with Basque lyrics, including "Euskadiko Neskak" (Basque Country Girls) and "Ai Ama" (Oh, Mother). "Ordago has helped the [cultural] transition [of Basques] into the eighties and nineties," said Morrie Berriochoa, the band's drummer. "Over in the Basque Country, an important part of the culture is the fiestas. And if we are playing a part to keep them alive here—our little 'fiestas'—then I guess we are, in a way, helping to keep the Basque community here together."[22] Gau Pasa, a group that played only Basque songs, also formed in the late 1990s and became a regular at Basque gatherings.

Perhaps the importance of music and dance to Basque culture was best demonstrated by the popularity of Boise'ko Gasteak, the dance group for Basque children from three to thirteen. Almost fifty years after Jay Hormaechea had begun her first lessons, more than 150 children were attending the weekly dancing and singing sessions. Older Basques and members of Oinkari volunteered to instruct the children, some of whom had only recently learned to walk. Just as they had in 1948, parents would stand in the back of the room and watch their children learn dance steps while they visited with other parents. "It's like [parents] are grasping for something," a longtime instructor commented. "They want their kids to have it. They want it so much. They don't want them to lose it."[23]

12

New Relations

lthough the pipeline of young Basques immigrating to the United States was running dry, the community in Idaho during the third generation had stronger relations than ever with the Basque Country—and, for the first time, stronger relations with other Basque communities scattered throughout the western United States. New links with Basques outside the state were invaluable in lending a sense of importance to maintaining Basque identity and to keeping the subculture in Idaho strong. Many young third-generation Basques would meet their counterparts from California or Donosti and feel, despite growing up in very different environments, that they shared something unique, something that they realized for the first time was vital to preserve. The informal contacts often kept young Basques in Idaho involved in Basque culture.

Until the third generation, Basques in Idaho had little contact with their kinsmen who had immigrated to other areas of the West. "We knew there was something out there, but we were not sure quite what," one Idaho Basque American said. Because most immigrants followed other family members or others from their hometown, patterns were established that remained in operation for decades. This, along with the distances and the deserts and mountain ranges between communities, allowed few opportunities for contact. The situation changed after Basques in Nevada organized the First National Basque Festival in 1959. Held outside Reno, this event was successful in attracting Basques throughout the West, partially because of its centralized location. In

1973, Basque representatives from clubs throughout the West met in Reno to form the North American Basque Organization (NABO).[1]

The new organization clearly demonstrated a desire for Basque Americans to stay in contact with other Basque Americans. NABO developed an organized calendar of activities to promote culture among all ages of Basques. One of its biggest successes was the annual Basque Music Camp, where youngsters learned Basque music, dancing, and other skills from Basque instructors. NABO organized handball and *mus* tournaments, and, on a broader level, held an annual convention, which was hosted by a different Basque club every year. This event attracted a large number of Basques from all areas of the United States. The NABO conventions were usually three-day affairs, with musical and dancing performances by groups from throughout the West and occasionally by groups from the Basque Country. The conventions also featured a mass, a public dance, sports competitions, and booths offering Basque food, artwork, and souvenirs.

Many Idaho Basques attended the convention festivals every summer. Through the conventions and other NABO activities Basques in Idaho could realize that they were part of a larger group and that Basques in other areas of the United States had formed strong communities of their own. They were often exposed to new traditions that thrived in other communities; some of those traditions had gone through their own transitions since arriving in this country from Euskadi. The festivalgoers watched dances they had never seen before and listened to new forms of Euskera that had the telltale inflections of the French Basque dialects. The younger participants often made friends with Basques from Nevada, Utah, and California, who offered them new inspiration to stay in touch with their subculture.

Besides forming stronger relations with other Basque Americans, Idaho Basques began to develop new ties with the Basque Country. Until the third generation, relations had been based primarily on ties with family; now, with the ease of travel and communication, the relations were becoming more social, academic, and even political. For American students who pursued studies in the Basque Country, Boise State University maintained an endowed scholarship foundation. Started in 1972 by the family of Lynne Fereday, a student who had died in an accident in Donosti, the scholarship awarded thirty thousand dollars to thirty-four students over the next twelve years. In 1984 the family of Domingo

Ansotegui combined efforts with the Feredays to create the Ansotegui-Fereday Memorial Scholarship, which benefited dozens of young Basques in Idaho. As had the Boise State University campus in Oñati, the University Consortium program in Donosti continued to reinvigorate Idaho's Basque community. Dozens of Basque Americans returned from their experiences committed to making the Basque culture an important part of their lives.[2]

Students were also traveling in the opposite direction, from Euskadi to Idaho. Though the improved Basque economy had ended immigration, by the 1980s there were increasing numbers of "short-term" immigrants—young Basques who visited the state to study English. They stayed with relatives or other Basque families, attended Idaho high schools or universities, and supplemented their academic experiences with a firm grasp of English—a valuable asset for finding employment back home. Many students became involved with the Idaho Basque community, joining the Oinkaris or at the very least attending local Basque picnics and dances. They were often quite surprised to see customs that had died out or were no longer widely popular in the Basque Country. One visitor remarked, "I did not know how to dance the jota until I spent a year in Idaho."[3]

Others traveled from Euskadi for short visits or for events such as Jaialdi, Boise's international Basque festival. Besides the usual events like a large dance and a mass, Jaialdi's schedule included aspects of Basque culture that were not normally a part of Basque festivals—a contemporary Basque cinema festival, a symposium featuring Basque scholars, and historical and artistic exhibits, among other activities. The large attendance and the number of artisans, athletes, musicians, and dancers from Euskadi were unprecedented in the United States. It was another form of exposure that Basque Americans had never had the opportunity to enjoy before.

Besides these social, cultural, and academic exchanges, the third generation witnessed a rise in political relations between Idaho and Euskadi. During the Franco era, there were no Basque politicians to bolster connections with the Basque diaspora in the Americas. After Basques were granted a degree of autonomy in the late 1970s, however, they gradually saw the advantages of maintaining contact with their overseas communities. One of the first formal visits came in 1981, when a delegation traveled to Idaho for the symbolic planting of a sapling from the

Tree of Gernika, the most significant symbol of Basque identity and democracy. The two delegates, Alberto Amorretu and José Manuel Sabala, joined Idaho governor John Evans in planting the foot-tall sapling on the statehouse lawn.

Other officials followed. In March 1988 the president of the Autonomous Government of the Basque Country, José Antonio Ardanza, stopped in Boise on a tour of the United States. The *lehendakari* (president) and his wife were greeted at the airport by a large crowd from the Basque community, including the Oinkari dancers and the Biotzetik choir. "The minute they stepped off the plane," recalled former governor Cecil Andrus, who was also at the airport, "they really captured the affection of the people." Ardanza spent several days in Boise visiting with the Basque community and meeting with local businessmen. He and his wife then traveled with Secretary of State Pete Cenarrusa for a short visit with President Reagan in the White House. After Ardanza's trip, Cecil Andrus said, "We were more aggressive in sending people to the Basque Country." Andrus himself visited Euskadi and addressed the Basque Parliament, as did Idaho's U.S. congressman Larry LaRocco in 1993. At the Sheepherders' Ball in 1992, Boise mayor Dirk Kempthorne read a proclamation declaring Boise and Gernika to be sister cities, in recognition of the large population from that city who had moved to the Boise area. Officials from both areas recognized that the strong tie of heritage could open a path for future commercial relations. In December 1992 the University of Idaho College of Agriculture undertook a trade mission to the Basque Country, where they agreed with Basque officials on a joint potato and sugar beet project.[4]

The increased political visits revealed how the Idaho Basque community—and its relations with the Basque Country—had changed over the decades. In 1937 exiled Basque government representative Manuel de Sota visited Idaho to seek financial support for war efforts but left empty-handed. More than fifty years later, President Ardanza visited Idaho to strengthen cultural ties with the offspring of those who had left the Basque Country in difficult times and to build on the sentiment that American-born Basques had for Euskadi. During his visit, Ardanza laid a large carnation wreath near a row of headstones in a section of Boise's Morris Hill cemetery, where hundreds of Basques had been buried over the years. "The Basques that came [to Idaho] transplanted in this land a seedling from the homeland," Ardanza said at the ceremony. "Perhaps it was one of the most beautiful seedlings of all."[5]

Down Grove Street

Just after the turn of the century, on a small plot on Grove Street in Boise, a Basque boardinghouse owner planted a vegetable garden to help supply food for the hungry crowd filling his tables. On the same site in the late 1940s, some first- and second-generation Basques constructed a no-frills building, the Basque Center, for cultural activities originally held in the boardinghouses. By 1972 Basques had given the building a face-lift, a stucco-and-beamed farmhouse facade resembling an Old World *baserri*. Grove Street, one of Boise's oldest streets, always seemed to mark changes in the Idaho Basque community; this was still evident at the end of the twentieth century when the development of a "Basque block" demonstrated a strong attempt at cultural preservation and, possibly, a glimpse of things to come.

The block was on the south side of Grove, between Sixth Street and Capitol Boulevard, offering a mixture of old and new. The Basque Center, built almost forty years earlier, still served as a gathering place for Basques for most social events. The Basque Center hosted the Sheepherders' Balls, the Basque Bazaar, countless Basque wedding receptions, and monthly Euzkaldunak dinners. In late fall one could still smell the strong odor of leeks near the center as Basques prepared thousands of sausages for the bazaar. It was not quite as crowded around the bar as it had been in the 1950s, but older immigrants still gathered daily for a few drinks and the promise of healthy argument. Younger Basques were frequent visitors, especially the Oinkaris, who still used the hall for their practice sessions.

Next door was the Basque Museum and Cultural Center. In the mid-1980s the museum's founder, Adelia Garro Simplot, acquired the red-brick house, which had been built in 1864 and operated for decades as a boardinghouse. She planned to make it a spot to preserve information about Basques' immigration to Idaho. In 1987 the building was dedicated, and an oak sapling from the Tree of Gernika was planted. The museum also acquired the building next door, which was remodeled to include a gift shop, an exhibition room, a library, and classrooms.

Older Basques volunteered to assist visitors in the main exhibition, which featured photographs of early immigrants and an actual sheep wagon as part of a display of the herding life. Schoolchildren from around the state were offered presentations on Basques in Idaho. Basque language courses for adults were also taught at night.

The goals of the Basque Museum and Cultural Center fulfilled Basques' desire for ethnic preservation. "We want to preserve and promote the history and study of the Basque culture in many forms, including its language, dances, and music," said Adelia Garro Simplot. In a turnaround from the mission of Basque insurance groups earlier in the century, many of which sought to help members Americanize, the museum pledged to stimulate "the development and offering of Basque literature, language studies, history"; the museum would serve as a center for "assembly and maintenance of a collection of Basque-related artifacts . . . in this state and elsewhere."[6] Although many had dismissed the study of Basque language, the museum sponsored a preschool *ikastola* for young children to learn Basque. Though still in its early stages, the *ikastola* could make a significant difference in Basque language use. On the block past the museum, the old Anduiza boardinghouse building, after decades of use as office space for various businesses, once again came into Basque ownership. The building's facade was renovated, and the Basque government has expressed interest in contributing to a more thorough restoration. The original fronton still stood, the chicken wire above pocked by balls lost to players decades earlier. The face-lift given the fronton in the early 1970s was crumbling, but there was hope that Basque sports might make a popular comeback with the formation of the Boise Fronton Association in the early 1990s.

At the corner of Grove and Capitol stood the Bar Gernika, founded in 1991 by Dan Ansotegui, a third-generation Basque who participated in the Oñati program and returned to the Basque Country several times. "I would never have opened up this kind of bar if I hadn't been to the Basque Country," he said. In the town of Gernika there was a Bar Boise, so it "seemed logical," he said, "that there should be a Bar Gernika in Boise." In many ways, the Bar Gernika became the Basque center for the younger generation, a place to gather on a regular basis with Basque friends. But it was frequented by non-Basques as well, from college students to state legislators taking a lunch break from their meetings in the nearby capitol. Bar Gernika offered a cozy hangout with an abundance of Old World flavor. "The design inside is a complete theft," Ansotegui said. "I stole the ideas from bars over there [in Euskadi]. I'd have a little notebook, and whenever I saw something I really liked, I wrote it down. Some of it's from a bar in Oñati, some from Donosti, from every bar I was in." Above the bar was a large collection of coffee cups, most from Basque bars. On the brick wall Ansotegui hung pictures from the Basque Country—photos of old farms, dancing groups, and rural picnics. He hung peppers, garlic, a jai alai basket, and the musical instruments his family has used for playing at gatherings and for the Oinkaris for over twenty-five years.[7]

Conclusion

Early observers of the Basque community in Idaho predicted a gloomy future for the survival of their culture. This seemed a reasonable prognostication at the time, because children of immigrants were Americanizing and discarding typical Basque cultural traits at a rapid pace. Basques seemed destined for the fate of most ethnic groups across the country, a gradual absorption into American society to the point where no ethnic traces other than unique surnames remained. But sixty years after this forecast, the Basque subculture in Idaho was far from obsolete; if anything, it seemed to be at a new peak. Boise's Basque block, the success of the Jaialdi festivals, the strong participation in music and dancing groups, and continuing exchanges between Idaho and the Basque Country—all seemed to indicate a steady pulse for the subculture.[8]

The Basques could point with pride to a vibrant celebration of this unique subculture. It lasted because from the day in 1889 when Antonio Azcuenaga and José Navarro staggered into Idaho, there had always been strong opportunities to survive, to succeed, and later, to be part of a heritage. America's clichéd description as "the Land of Opportunity" was accurate for many Basques, who first came to Idaho in order to escape a lack of opportunity back home and who, like other immigrants to the United States, gladly took the lowest jobs available in the new land. They in turn created opportunities for their descendants, the chance to make a successful entry in American society and still be part of something larger, a community and a rich tradition.

The subculture survived because, through the years, Basques have been able to change it along with the times. "Culture is a human institu-

tion," remarked one third-generation Basque. "We create it as we go."
Over time in Idaho Basques evolved, changed old habits and traditions,
adapted to new ways of thinking and living. American-born Basques
found ways of ethnic expression while they held jobs as bankers or lawyers, choosing enjoyable outlets that allowed them to maintain close
personal friendships with other Basque Americans. The third generation formed a larger number of cultural organizations than ever, dem-
onstrating an awakened interest in the search for roots, along with the
necessity to institutionalize ethnicity in order to save it.[9]

The Basque subculture thrived in Idaho because the state helped
make it possible. Idahoans were glad to hire Basque immigrants, especially because the work they were willing to do was work nobody else
wanted. Whatever early prejudices and suspicions Idahoans carried were
transformed into a high regard for the Basques, for their reputation as
hard workers who also knew how to have a good time. They came to respect Basques for their ability to combine pride in their ethnicity along
with pride as Americans. At most Basque festivals, an American flag
hangs beside the Basque *ikurrina,* and at the opening ceremonies of
these festivals participants often sing both the American and the Basque
anthems. In many ways Idaho, a rural state with few unified ethnic
groups, looks at the Basques' success as one of its own successes. The
same Caldwell newspaper that in 1909 labeled Basques as "dirty, itinerant, clannish, black Bascos" had kinder comments by the end of the
century: "Basque blood runs strong in even the second or third generations," the paper claimed. "A Basque will always be a Basque—proud,
vigorous and self-confident even if he is an American. And America is
so much richer for it."[10]

This ethnic pride could be the biggest reason that the culture lasted.
Although there was a relatively large concentration of Basques in Idaho,
there were few of them around the world. Because of this, and because
of the constant historical challenges they had to face in order to maintain their identity, Basques are unusually proud and determined to be
so. An elderly Basque remembered his grandfather pointing to a bridge
constructed in the Basque region by the Romans. "They're long gone,"
his grandfather told him, "but we're still here." This was passed on like
a gene to many descendants of Basque immigrants worldwide. "When
you know somebody is Basque, you just have a different relationship
with them," one Basque American said. "You have something in com-

mon by virtue of your blood. It really doesn't matter if that is the only thing you share."[11]

This common bond of being Basque lasted over the century despite the changes in what it meant to "be Basque." Decades of social change and intermarriage have blurred Basque identity. Being Basque, for some, means having a Basque surname. For others, it means involvement in some aspect of Basque culture, some outward form of ethnic expression. "I don't care if he's at a dance wearing a *txapela* ass-backwards," one Boise Basque said. "To me, that person is Basque."[12]

Many contributions to the survival of the Basque subculture in Idaho have been made by individuals with no Basque heritage at all, those who through marriage or curiosity were introduced to Basque culture and became heavily involved. Some of these non-Basques contributed as much or more to the continuation of Idaho's Basque community as anyone else. One of the main organizers of the Jaialdi festivals had no Basque heritage; neither did the director of the Boise State University program in Oñati; a longtime Oinkari musician; or the director (and many members) of the Biotzetik Basque Choir. A unique ethnic multiplication took place, because someone with a connection to the Basque community could make it possible for many others to become involved. A woman of one-quarter Basque heritage could marry a non-Basque man, drawing him, and later their children, into the fold.

This connection highlighted the importance and convenience of choice. Choice has always been at the heart of the Basque community in Idaho. The immigrants chose to move to Idaho, then chose to stay. Later, their descendants would choose whether they wanted to "be Basque." By the third generation, these individual choices seem more important than ever with respect to maintaining a Basque subculture in Idaho. Many "Basques" of full, half, one-quarter, or zero Basque heritage were devoting a large portion of their free time to maintaining the resurgence that had developed. The Basque experience illustrated Marcus Lee Hansen's third-generations theory—things that are not important to the child of immigrants often become vital to the grandchild.[13]

What will be important—and how long it will continue to be important—will probably change for future generations, those who grow up without Old World relatives but who will have easier, more convenient travel and communication opportunities. "I have no doubt that [Idaho's Basque subculture] will continue," a third-generation Boise

Basque said. "There are a lot of young people involved. The festivals are well attended. This is going to last at least through our lifetimes and probably through our kids'. But the question then becomes, 'What is *this* going to be?'" As in the 1930s, predictions are challenging. Some smaller Basque communities in Idaho—in Mountain Home, Gooding, and Caldwell, for example—continue to sponsor Basque events. But participation in other towns seems to be eroding. Even though hundreds of children continue to learn Basque music and dancing, it is impossible to know if they will stay involved later. Jaialdi festivals are hugely successful in keeping Basques tuned in to their subculture, providing a large occasional reminder of the community they had. But it is also impossible to know if future generations will choose to dedicate the time and energy that is necessary to organize the festivals. There is a potential for an upsurge in the study of Basque language, with improved communication and study programs, but if the past is any indication, it seems difficult to imagine that great-grandchildren of immigrants will find it worth their time.[14]

Available opportunities and subsequent choices will determine whether the Basque subculture in Idaho continues to thrive or whether the third generation represents a period of "Indian summer," with signs of winter soon approaching. What cultural traits survive and what new ones will be created depend, as always, on the choices that later generations make.

Epilogue

Frank and Frances Bilbao traveled to the Basque Country in March 1991 for what was intended to be their last trip. They were accompanied by all three of their children—Dolores, Julio, and Frankie. They were going to visit the Basque Country one more time and to see Josie, who was teaching English in an academy in Ondarroa, Bizkaia. They traveled in Bizkaia, visiting with Frank's family in Ondarroa, touring small coastal towns like Bermeo. They did not stray far from the region where Frank had grown up and where Frances's family had come from.

One afternoon they decided to visit San Juan de Gastelugatxe, the beautiful chapel on the cliff top where decades earlier Frank had worked for sixteen dollars a year, climbing the 365 steps to the top so he could clean the chapel and cut the grass from the slopes.

They drove the curvy road to San Juan de Gastelugatxe, proceeding until the path stopped at the base of the hill. Everyone got out of the car and began the long trek. But Frank decided to stay behind, feeling that the climb was too high for him.

He watched his children walk up the 365 steps to the chapel so they could get a view of the ocean from up high. "I stood there watching them, and I could hardly believe it, thinking I used to cut that grass all the way up there. I could hardly believe I worked that hard."

NOTES

INTRODUCTION

1. Sol Silen, *La historia de los Vascongados en el oeste de los Estados Unidos* (New York: Las Novedades, 1917), 182–83.

2. Jose Mari Artiach, interview by authors, 10 June 1993.

3. Marcus Lee Hansen, "The Third Generation: Search for Continuity," in *Children of the Uprooted*, ed. Oscar Handlin (Englewood, N.J.: Prentice-Hall, 1959).

ONE. AN ANCIENT PEOPLE

1. William A. Douglass and Jon Bilbao, *Amerikanuak: Basques in the New World* (Reno: University of Nevada Press, 1975), 10–11.

2. Robert P. Clark, *The Basques: The Franco Years and Beyond* (Reno: University of Nevada Press, 1979), 15.

3. Ibid., 328–38.

4. John Hooper, *The Spaniards: A Portrait of the New Spain* (Harmondsworth, Middlesex, England, and New York: Penguin Books, 1987), 217; also, Evan Hadingham, "Europe's Mystery People," *World Monitor Magazine* (September 1992): 36.

5. Hooper, *The Spaniards*.

6. Clark, *The Basques,* 11; Stanley Payne, *Basque Nationalism* (Reno: University of Nevada Press, 1975), 10.

7. From Rachel Bard, "Aimery Picaud and the Basques: Selections from the *Pilgrim's Guide to Santiago de Compostela*," in *Essays in Basque Social Anthropology and History,* ed. William A. Douglass (Reno: Basque Studies Program, University of Nevada, Reno, 1989), 203.

8. Douglass and Bilbao, *Amerikanuak,* 45; Hooper, *The Spaniards,* 220; Clark, *The Basques,* 15.

9. Payne, *Basque Nationalism,* 26–27; John Adams, *A Defense of the Constitution of the Government of the United States.*

10. Hadingham, "Europe's Mystery People," 34–40; Douglass and Bilbao, *Amerikanuak,* 67–68.

11. Payne, *Basque Nationalism,* 40–53; Hooper, *The Spaniards,* 224.

12. Payne, *Basque Nationalism,* 52.

13. Clark, *The Basques,* 25.

14. Payne, *Basque Nationalism,* 75; Hooper, *The Spaniards,* 225.

15. Payne, *Basque Nationalism.*

16. Clark, *The Basques,* 40–46.

17. Ibid.

18. William A. Douglass, "Serving Girls and Sheepherders: Emigration and Continuity in a Spanish Basque Village," in *The Changing Faces of Rural Spain,* ed. Joseph B. Aceves and William A. Douglass (New York: Schenkman Publishing, Halstead Press Division, John Wiley, 1976), 48; Hooper, *The Spaniards,* 222; Joe Eiguren, interviews by authors, 4 December 1991, 18 February 1992, 24 March 1993.

19. Douglass, "Serving Girls and Sheepherders," 48.

20. Ibid.

21. Eiguren interview, 24 March 1993.

22. Douglass, "Serving Girls and Sheepherders," 49.

23. Eiguren interview, 18 February 1992.

24. William A. Douglass, "The Basques of the American West: Preliminary Historical Perspectives," *Nevada Historical Quarterly* 13, no. 4 (Winter 1970): 14; Pat Bieter, "Reluctant Sheepherders: The Basques in Idaho," *Idaho Yesterdays* 1, no. 2 (Summer 1957): 5.

25. Douglass, "Serving Girls and Sheepherders," 49.

26. Marie Pierre Arrizabalaga, "A Statistical Study of Basque Immigration into California, Nevada, Idaho and Wyoming, 1900–1910" (master's thesis, University of Nevada, Reno, September 1986), 29.

27. Eiguren interview, 4 December 1991.

28. *Idaho Statesman,* 20 May 1928.

29. William A. Douglass, interview by authors, 4 August 1993, Reno, Nevada.

30. Hadingham, "Europe's Mystery People," 37.

31. Douglass and Bilbao, *Amerikanuak,* 72.

32. Ibid., 139–68.

33. Richard W. Etulain, "Basque Beginnings in the Pacific Northwest," *Idaho Yesterdays* 18, no. 1 (Spring 1974): 26.

34. Douglass and Bilbao, *Amerikanuak,* 135; Ethel A. Roesch, "Basques of the Sawtooth Range," *Frontier Times* (April–May 1964): 14.

35. *Idaho Statesman,* 8 May 1949; Julio Bilbao, "Basque Names in Early Idaho," *Idaho Yesterdays* 15 (Summer 1971): 26–29.

36. Sol Silen, *La Historia de los vascongados en el oeste de los Estados Unidos* (New York: Las Novedades, 1917), 83.

37. Douglass interview.

38. Ibid.

TWO. THE TRIP TO IDAHO

1. Franklin D. Scott, *The Peopling of America: Perspectives on Immigration* (Washington, D.C.: American Historical Association Pamphlets, 1963), 27, 31.

2. Marie Pierre Arrizabalaga, "A Statistical Study of Basque Immigration into California, Nevada, Idaho and Wyoming, 1900–1910" (master's thesis, University of Nevada, Reno, September 1986), 88–92.

3. Jose Solasabal, interview by authors; Pat Bieter, "John Archabal and the American Basques" (unpublished paper, 1956), 9.

4. Lucy Garatea, interview by authors, 7 February 1992; Oscar Israelowitz, *Ellis Island Guide* (Brooklyn, N.Y.: Israelowitz Publishing, 1990), 14–20.

5. Regina Bastida, interview by authors; William A. Douglass and Jon Bilbao, *Amerikanuak: Basques in the New World* (Reno: University of Nevada Press, 1975), 374.

6. Bieter, "Reluctant Shepherds: The Basques in Idaho," *Idaho Yesterdays* 1, no. 2 (Summer 1957): 13.

7. John B. Edlefsen, "A Sociological Study of the Basques of Southwest Idaho" (Ph.D. diss., State College of Washington, 1948), 48–49.

8. Merle Wells, *Boise: An Illustrated History* (Woodland Hills, Calif.: Windsor Publications, 1982), 43–79.

9. Ibid.

10. Garmendia letters, Basque Museum and Cultural Center, Boise, Idaho.

11. Regina Bastida interview.

12. 1909 Boise City Directory (Boise: Statesman Printing Company, 1909); James H. Hawley, *History of Idaho: The Gem of the Mountains,* vol. 3 (Chicago: Clarke Publishing, 1920), 760; Sol Silen, *La Historia de los vascongados en el oeste de los Estados Unidos* (New York: Las Novedades, 1917), 183.

13. Douglass and Bilbao, *Amerikanuak,* 331.

14. Edward Wentworth, *America's Sheep Trails: History, Personalities* (Ames: Iowa State College Press, 1948), 286–94; Idaho Wool Growers Association statistics.

15. Ethel A. Roesch, "Basques of the Sawtooth Range," *Frontier Times* (April–May 1964): 15; Archer B. Gilfillan, *Sheep* (Boston: Little, Brown, 1930), 4–5.

16. Joe Eiguren, interviews by authors, 4 December 1991, 18 February 1992, 24 March 1993; Wentworth, *America's Sheep Trails,* 290.

17. Sabino Landa, interview by authors, 18 March 1992.

18. Ibid.; William A. Douglass, "The Basques of the American West: Preliminary Historical Perspectives," *Nevada Historical Quarterly* 13, no. 4 (Winter 1970): 21.

19. Douglass and Bilbao, *Amerikanuak,* 229; Gilfillan, *Sheep,* 3; Elmore County Criminal Records, *State of Idaho v. Martin Ancenechea.*

20. Garmendia letters.

21. Frank Bilbao, interview by authors, Cascade, Idaho, 9 February 1991.

22. Tom Keelan, "With the Miners Came the Sheep," *Boise Idaho Statesman Centennial Supplement* (1990): 2.

23. Idaho State Court Records, *State of Idaho v. Yturaspe* (1911).

24. United States Supreme Court Records, *Omaechevarria v. State of Idaho* (1917).

25. *Caldwell Tribune,* 17 July 1909, 4.

26. Nick Beristain, interview by authors, 20 March 1992; Eiguren interview, 4 December 1991; Mike Hanley, with Ellis Lucia, *Owyhee Trails: The West's Forgotten Corner* (Caldwell, Idaho: Caxton Printers, 1973), 268; and Lydia Lachiondo, interview by authors, 17 July 1992.

27. Grant E. McCall, "Basque-Americans and a Sequential Theory of Migration and Adaptation" (master's thesis, San Francisco State College, 1968), 83.

28. Louise Shaddock, *Andy Little: Idaho Sheep King* (Caldwell, Idaho: Caxton Printers, 1990), 129.

29. *National Wool Grower* 35, no. 12 (December 1945): 33.

30. Garmendia letters; Pete Cenarrusa, interview by authors, 9 June 1993.

31. Douglass and Bilbao, *Amerikanuak,* 299.

32. *Idaho Statesman,* 7 October 1925, 2.

33. Jose Mari Artiach, interview by authors, 10 June 1993.

THREE. BOARDINGHOUSES

1. Ada County Naturalization Records; William A. Douglass and Jon Bilbao, *Amerikanuak: Basques in the New World* (Reno: University of Nevada Press, 1975), 379.

2. Richard W. Etulain, "Basque Beginnings in the Pacific Northwest," *Idaho Yesterdays* 18, no. 1 (Spring 1974): 30; Marie Pierre Arrizabalaga, "A Statistical Study of Basque Immigration into California, Nevada, Idaho and Wyoming, 1900–1910" (master's thesis, University of Nevada, Reno, September 1986), 89.

3. Garmendia letters, Basque Museum and Cultural Center.

4. Douglass and Bilbao, *Amerikanuak,* 379; Pat Bieter, "Letemendi's Boarding House," *Idaho Yesterdays* 37 (Spring 1993): 3.

5. "Shoshone and Idaho Perspectives" booklet (Boise: Idaho Humanities Council, 1990), 26.

6. Luis Arrizabala, "Jaialdi '90 International Basque Festival Cultural Program Book," 64–83.

7. Boise City Directory, 1909–1910; Arthur Hart, *Life in Old Boise* (Boise: Historic Idaho, Inc., and Boise City Celebrations, 1989), 185; John Anduiza, interview by authors, Boise, Idaho, 21 March 1992.

8. Nick Beristain, interviews by authors, 20 March 1992, 7 June 1993.

9. Ibid.

10. Bieter, "Letemendi's," 4; Arrizabala, "Jaialdi '90."

11. Ibid.

12. Anduiza interview.

13. Garmendia letters.

14. Arrizabala, "Jaialdi '90"; Robert S. Smith, *Doctors and Patients* (Boise: Syms York, 1968), 115–16.

15. Stack Yribar, interview by authors, 2 February 1992.

16. *Idaho Statesman,* 30 April 1960; Socorros Mutuos bylaws; Douglass and Bilbao, *Amerikanuak,* 299, 384–85.

17. Henry Alegria, *75 Years of Memoirs* (Caldwell, Idaho: Caxton Printers, 1981), 23; Richard Urquidi, "History of the Mountain Home Basques" (master's thesis, Boise State University, 1980), 8.

18. Lucy Garatea, interview by authors, 7 February 1992.

19. Juanita Hormaechea, interviews by authors, 28 September 1991 and 6 July 1993.

20. Paquita Garatea, "Burnseko Etxekoandreak: Basque Women Boarding House Keepers of Burns, Oregon" (master's thesis, Portland State University, 1990), 29; Garatea interview.

21. Garatea interview.

22. John and Regina Bastida, Garatea, and Hormaechea interviews.

23. Ibid.

24. Bastida and Hormaechea interviews.

25. Bieter, "Letemendi's," 6; Beristain interview, 7 June 1993.

26. Douglass and Bilbao, *Amerikanuak,* 377; Jeronima Echevarria, "Ostatuak Amerikanuak: A History of Basque-American Boardinghouses" (unpublished paper), 6.

27. John and Regina Bastida interview.

28. Yribar interview.

29. Garatea interview.

30. Ibid.

31. Hormaechea interview; Marie Uriarte, interview by authors, 14 July 1993.

32. John B. Edlefsen, "A Sociological Study of the Basques of Southwest Idaho" (Ph.D. diss., State College of Washington, 1948), 65.

FOUR. IDAHOANS GET TO KNOW THE BASQUES

1. Henry Alegria, *75 Years of Memoirs* (Caldwell, Idaho: Caxton Printers, 1981), 141–42.

2. John Anduiza, interview by authors, 21 March 1992.

3. Alegria, *75 Years ,* 130.

4. *Idaho Statesman,* 19 June 1978.

5. Ibid., 1 January 1949.

6. Jeronima Echevarria, "Ostatuak Amerikanuak: A History of Basque-American Boardinghouses" (unpublished paper), 7.

7. Joseph Harold Gaiser, "The Basques of Jordan Valley: A Study of Social Process and Social Change" (Ph.D. diss., University of Southern California, 1944), 39; Pat Bieter, "Reluctant Herders: The Basques in Idaho," *Idaho Yesterdays* 1, no. 2 (Summer 1957): 13.

8. John B. Edlefsen, "A Sociological Study of the Basques of Southwest Idaho" (Ph.D. diss., State College of Washington, 1948), 68; Juanita Hormaechea, interviews by authors, 28 September 1991, 6 June 1993.

9. Hormaechea interview; Marie Uriarte, interview by authors, 14 July 1993.

10. Anduiza interview; Nick Beristain, interviews by authors, 20 March 1992, 7 June 1993.

11. Garmendia letters, Basque Museum and Cultural Center.

12. Arthur Hart, *Life in Old Boise* (Boise: Historic Idaho, Inc., and Boise City Celebrations, 1989), 83–84; Lydia Lachiondo, interview by authors, July 1992.

13. William A. Douglass and Jon Bilbao, *Amerikanuak: Basques in the New World* (Reno: University of Nevada Press, 1975), 376; Stack Yribar, interview by authors, 2 February 1992.

14. John Ysursa, interview by authors, 30 July 1993; Julie Abraham, interview by authors, 25 March 1992.

15. Uriarte interview; Richard Urquidi, "History of the Mountain Home Basques" (master's thesis, Boise State University, 1980), 45.

16. *Idaho Daily Statesman,* 10 March 1911, 7.

17. Beristain and Hormaechea interviews; Socorros Mutuos bylaws.

18. Rodney Gallop, *A Book of the Basques* (Reno: University of Nevada Press, 1970), 54; Joe Eiguren, interviews by authors, 4 December 1991, 18 February 1992, 24 March 1993.

19. Eiguren interviews, 18 February 1992 and 24 March 1993.

20. Edlefsen, "A Sociological Study," 99–100; Douglass, interview by authors, 4 August 1993, Reno, Nevada.

21. Father Peplinski, interview by authors, 19 March 1992; Gaiser, "The Basques of Jordan Valley," 68.

22. *Boise Catholic Monthly,* March 1919; *Idaho Statesman,* 3 March 1919.

23. Cyprian Bradley and Edward J. Kelly, "History of the Diocese of Boise" (unpublished manuscript, 1942), sec. 3.

24. *Boise Catholic Monthly,* March 1919.

25. Asuncion Ysursa, interview by authors, 18 March 1992; Gallop, *Book of the Basques,* 230.

26. Franklin, "The Peopling of America," 48.

27. Ibid., 51–52; Douglass and Bilbao, *Amerikanuak,* 305.

28. Hart, *Life in Old Boise,* 84–86.

29. Ibid.; Ethnic Heritage Historical Overviews, 18–37, 70–76.

30. Edlefsen, "A Sociological Study," 56; Gaiser, "The Basques of Jordan Valley," 42.

31. James H. Hawley, *History of Idaho: The Gem of the Mountains,* vol. 3 (Chicago: Clarke Publishing, 1920), 101–2.

32. Ethel A. Roesch, "Basques of the Sawtooth Range," *Frontier Times* (April–May 1964): 15.

33. *Idaho Statesman,* 8 June 1928.

FIVE. INTO THE CRUCIBLE

1. Rodney Gallop, *A Book of the Basques* (Reno: University of Nevada Press, 1970), 60.

2. Zangwill, 33.

3. Henry Alegria, *75 Years of Memoirs* (Caldwell, Idaho: Caxton Printers, 1981), 18; John B. Edlefsen, "A Sociological Study of the Basques of Southwest Idaho" (Ph.D. diss., State College of Washington, 1948), 78.

4. Articles of Incorporation of the American Basque Fraternity, 10 December 1928, 2.

5. Edlefsen, "A Sociological Study," 55; Jaialdi '87 booklet.

6. Jaialdi '90 booklet.

7. *Idaho Statesman,* October 1931.

8. William A. Douglass, interview by authors, Reno, Nevada, 4 August 1993; Edlefsen, "A Sociological Study," 46; Eloise Bieter, interview by authors, 12 February 1992.

9. Garmendia letters, Basque Museum and Cultural Center; *Idaho Statesman,* 27 January 1941; John Anduiza, interview by authors, 21 March 1992.

10. Uriarte, interview by authors, 14 July 1993.

11. Joseph Harold Gaiser, "The Basques of Jordan Valley: A Study in Social Process and Social Change" (Ph.D. diss., University of Southern California, 1944), 55; Lydia Lachiondo, interview by authors, 19 July 1992.

12. Lachiondo interview; Jimmy Jausoro, interview by authors, 15 October 1991.

13. Dave Eiguren, interview by authors, 8 April 1993; Toni Achabal, interviews by authors, 22 March 1993 and 13 May 1993.

14. Gaiser, "The Basques of Jordan Valley: A Study in Social Process and Social Change," 179; *Idaho Statesman,* 27 January 1941.

15. Ibid.

16. Edlefsen, "A Sociological Study," 103–6.

17. *Idaho Statesman,* 25 November 1937.

18. *Lewiston Morning Tribune,* 1958.

SIX. THE DECLINE OF BASQUE ENTRY AND CULTURE

1. Nick Beristain, interviews by authors, 20 March 1992 and 7 June 1993.

2. Ibid.

3. Richard Urquidi, "History of the Mountain Home Basques" (master's thesis, Boise State University, 1980), 10.

4. Ibid., 11.

5. Ibid., 12.

6. Dan Archabal, interview by authors, 2 August 1995.

7. Rosie Dick, interview by authors, 20 February 1992; La Organisación Independiente Sociale Bylaws, 7–11; Anes Mendiola, interview by authors, 13 February 1992; Idaho Humanities Council and the Idaho Centennial Commission, "Women's Organizations in Idaho" (1990), 4–5.

8. William A. Douglass and Jon Bilbao, *Amerikanuak: Basques in the New World* (Reno: University of Nevada Press, 1975), 282–97.

9. Ibid.; Catherine A. Kilher and Charles P. Koch, *Sheep and Man* (Denver: American Sheep Producers Council, 1978), 131.

10. Douglass and Bilbao, *Amerikanuak,* 294.

11. *Idaho Statesman,* 28 June–2 July 1937.

12. Ibid.

13. Ibid.

14. John B. Edlefsen, "A Sociological Study of the Basques of Southwest Idaho" (Ph.D. diss., State College of Washington, 1948), 67.

15. Articles of Incorporation, Independent Order of Spanish-Basque Speaking People of Idaho; Edlefsen, "A Sociological Study," 107.

16. Cyprian Bradley and Edward J. Kelly, "History of the Diocese of Boise" (unpublished paper, 1942), sec. 3.

17. Edlefsen, "A Sociological Study," 71.

18. Ibid., 93; Clifford A. Sather, "Marriage Patterns Among the Basques of Shoshone" (B.A. thesis, Reed College, 1961), 33; Marjorie Archabal, interview by authors, 19 June 1995.

19. Sather, "Marriage Patterns," 34.

20. Joseph Harold Gaiser, "The Basques of Jordan Valley: A Study in Social Process and Social Change" (Ph.D. diss., University of Southern California, 1944), 75; Edlefsen, "A Sociological Study," 123.

21. *Capital News*, 28 June 1937; Edlefsen, "A Sociological Study," 123; John Anduiza, interview by authors, 21 March 1992; L. S. Cressman and Anthony Yturri, "The Basques in Oregon," *Commonwealth Review* (March 1938): 367.

22. Cressman and Yturri, "The Basques in Oregon," 368.

SEVEN. WARTIME

1. Robert P. Clark, *The Basques: The Franco Years and Beyond* (Reno: University of Nevada Press, 1979), 48.

2. Stanley Payne, *Basque Nationalism* (Reno: University of Nevada Press, 1975), 163.

3. Clark, *The Basques,* 52–53.

4. Payne, *Basque Nationalism,* 163.

5. Clark, *The Basques,* 62, 64.

6. Ibid., 69.

7. Payne, *Basque Nationalism,* 183.

8. Clark, *The Basques,* 70.

9. Ibid.

10. Ibid., 83.

11. Payne, *Basque Nationalism,* 190.

12. Ibid., 191.

13. Clark, *The Basques,* 87.

14. Arsen Alzola, "The Basque Experience" (Murphy, Idaho: Owyhee County Historical Society, 1982), 5.

15. Joe Eiguren, interviews by authors, 4 December 1991, 18 February 1992, 24 March 1993.

16. William A. Douglass, interview by authors, 4 August 1993, Reno, Nevada.

17. *Idaho Statesman*, 31 July 1937; William A. Douglass and Jon Bilbao, *Amerikanuak: Basques in the New World* (Reno: University of Nevada Press, 1975), 361.

18. *Boise Capitol News,* 19 December 1937.

19. Douglass interview; *Boise Capitol News,* 20 December 1937.

20. Koldo San Sebastian, *The Basque Archives: Vascos en Estados Unidos (1938–1943)* (San Sebastián: Editorial Txertroa, n.d.), 171.

21. *Idaho Statesman,* 25 November 1940.

22. Juanita Hormaechea, interviews by authors, 28 September 1991, 6 July 1993.

23. Philip Gleason, "American Identity and Americanization," in *Harvard Encyclopedia of American Ethnic Groups,* ed. Stephen Thernstrom (Cambridge: Harvard University Press, 1980), 47.

24. *Idaho Statesman,* 2 December 1991; Joe Eiguren, *Kashpar* (Caldwell, Idaho: Caxton Printers, 1986), 66.

25. *Idaho Statesman,* 26 February 1945.

26. Ibid., 17 December 1942.

27. Dan Bilbao, telephone interview by authors to San Francisco, 17 January 1992; Stack Yribar, interview by authors, 2 February 1992.

28. Joseph Harold Gaiser, "The Basques of Jordan Valley: A Study in Social Process and Social Change" (Ph.D. diss., University of Southern California, 1944), 184; *Idaho Statesman,* 17 December 1942.

29. Gaiser, "The Basques of Jordan Valley," 184; *Idaho Statesman,* 26 February 1945.

EIGHT. A SUBCULTURE IS BORN

1. Angela Larrinaga, interview by authors, 4 September 1993, Boise, Idaho; Pete Cenarrusa, interview by authors, 9 June 1993.

2. Juanita Hormaechea, interviews by authors, 28 September 1991, 6 July 1993.

3. Jimmy Jausoro, interview by authors, 15 October 1991.

4. Jausoro interview; Larrinaga interview.

5. Disputes continued even within organizations. On 9 January 1937, members of the American Basque Fraternity filed a suit in Ada County District Court alleging that the organization leadership mismanaged the organization and violated the provisions of the articles of incorporation. *Idaho Statesman,* 9 January 1937, 20 February 1937, 6 April 1937.

6. Stack Yribar, interview by authors, 2 February 1992; William A. Douglass and Jon Bilbao, *Amerikanuak: Basques in the New World* (Reno: University of Nevada Press, 1975), 387.

7. *Boise Capitol News,* 19 December 1936.

8. John B. Edlefsen, "A Sociological Study of the Basques of Southwest Idaho" (Ph.D. diss., State College of Washington, 1948), 150.

9. William A. Douglass, "The Vanishing Basque Sheepherder," *American West* 17 (July–August 1980): 60; *Idaho Statesman,* 7 January 1947.

10. Ibid.

11. *Idaho Wool Growers Bulletin,* January 30, 1952.

12. Nick Beristain, interviews by authors, 20 March 1992, 7 June 1993.

13. *Idaho Statesman,* 7 October 1989; Jose Mari Artiach, interview by authors, 10 June 1993.

14. *Idaho Statesman,* 15 February 1928; Albert Erquiaga, interviews by authors, 11 November 1991, 13 May 1993; *Boise Capitol News,* 19 December 1936.

15. Joseph Harold Gaiser, "The Basques of Jordan Valley: A Study in Social Process and Social Change" (Ph.D. diss., University of Southern California, 1944), 118; Bernice Brusen, *Basques from the Pyrenees to the Rockies* (Portland, Ore.: Dynagraphics, 1985), 5.

16. Hormaechea interview.

17. Ibid.

18. *Idaho Statesman,* 17 December 1948.

19. Ibid.; Hormaechea interview.

20. Larrinaga interview.

21. *Idaho Statesman,* 9 May 1949.

22. Ibid.; Larrinaga interview.

23. *Idaho Statesman,* 9–10 May 1949.

24. Ibid.

NINE. THE OINKARI BASQUE DANCERS

1. Albert Erquiaga, interviews by authors, 11 November 1991, 13 May 1993; Simon Achabal and Toni Achabal, interviews by authors, 13 May 1993.

2. Ibid.

3. *Idaho Statesman,* 16 February 1964.

4. *Congressional Record,* 26 June 1964.

5. *Idaho Statesman,* 8 May 1964.

6. Erquiaga interview, 15 December 1991.

7. Marcus Lee Hansen, "The Third Generation: Search for Continuity," in *Children of the Uprooted,* ed. Oscar Handlin (Englewood, N.J.: Prentice-Hall, 1959), 43–46.

8. Philip Gleason, "American Identity and Americanization," in *Harvard Encyclopedia of American Ethnic Groups,* ed. Stephen Thernstrom (Cambridge: Harvard University Press, 1980), 54.

9. Michael Novak, *The Rise of the Unmeltable Ethnics* (New York: Macmillan, 1971), 115.

10. Oscar Handlin, ed., *Children of the Uprooted* (New York: G. Braziller, 1966), 85.

11. Novak, *The Rise of the Unmeltable Ethnics,* 108–10.

12. Herbert J. Gans, "Symbolic Ethnicity: The Future of Ethnic Groups and Cultures in America," *Ethnic and Racial Studies* (January 1979): 1.

13. Joe Eiguren, interviews by authors, 4 December 1991, 18 February 1992, 24 March 1993; *Idaho Statesman,* 13 September 1963.

14. Eiguren interviews.

15. Julio Bilbao, interview by authors, 21 June 1993; *Idaho Statesman,* 3 July 1960.

16. Idaho Basque Studies Grant Proposal.

17. *Idaho Statesman,* 26 December 1971.

18. Ibid., 9 June 1972.

19. Julio Bilbao interview; Josie Bilbao, interview by authors, 15 June 1993.

TEN. THE MODERN BASQUE COUNTRY

1. Pat Bieter, interviews by authors, 10 March 1992, 13 July 1993.

2. Ibid.

3. Jesus Alcelay, interview by authors, 19 July 1993.

4. Dan Ansotegui, interview by authors, 11 March 1992.

5. Josie Bilbao, interview by authors, 15 June 1993.

6. Pat Bieter interviews; Steve Mendive, interview by authors, 29 June 1993.

7. Dan Ansotegui interview.

8. John Ysursa, interview by authors, 30 July 1993.

9. Robert P. Clark, *The Basques: The Franco Years and Beyond* (Reno: University of Nevada Press, 1979), 80–81.

10. Ibid., 202–22.

11. Ibid.

12. Ibid., 130.

13. Ibid., 150.

14. *New York Times,* 20 December 1970.

15. Clark, *The Basques,* 182–87.

16. *Idaho Statesman,* 30 December 1970.

17. Justo Sarria, interview by authors, 10 March 1992.

18. Richard W. Etulain and Jeronima Echeverria, *Portraits of Basques in the New World* (Reno: University of Nevada Press, 1999), 172–91.

19. Ibid.

20. *Idaho Statesman,* 6 October 1975.

21. Frank Church news releases, 31 August 1968, 16 March 1977.

22. Bethine Church, interview by authors, 6 July 1993.

23. Ibid.

24. *Idaho Statesman,* 12 October 1975.

25. William A. Douglass and Jon Bilbao, *Amerikanuak: Basques in the New World* (Reno: University of Nevada Press, 1975), 322–23.

26. *Idaho Statesman,* 21 August 1962.

27. Ibid., 19 July 1952.

28. Ibid., 2 October 1970.

29. Nick Beristain, interviews by authors, 20 March 1992, 7 June 1993.

30. Jose Mari Artiach, interview by authors, 10 June 1993.

31. *Idaho Statesman,* 30 July 1953, 21 August 1962.

ELEVEN. THE END OF AN ERA

1. Lino Zabala, interview by authors, 5 June 1993.

2. Jose Mari Artiach, interview by authors, 10 June 1993.

3. Ibid.

4. *Idaho Wool Growers Bulletin,* 14 February 1951; *Idaho Statesman,* 26 May 1970.

5. William A. Douglass and Jon Bilbao, *Amerikanuak: Basques in the New World* (Reno: University of Nevada Press, 1975), 323.

6. *Idaho Statesman,* 19 July 1972.

7. Robert P. Clark, *The Basques: The Franco Years and Beyond* (Reno: University of Nevada Press, 1979), 46.

8. Ibid., 48.

9. Linda Barrinaga, interview by authors, 19 July 1993.

10. William A. Douglass, interview by authors, 4 August 1993, Reno, Nevada.

11. Bernard Lazerwitz and Louis Rowitz, "The Three Generations Hypothesis," *American Journal of Sociology* 69 (June 1964): 529; Steve Achabal, interview by authors, 13 April 1990.

12. Aucutt and Urquidi interviews.

13. Dan Ansotegui, interview by authors, 11 March 1992.

14. Ron Lemmon, interview by authors, 15 March 1992.

15. Albert Erquiaga, interviews by authors, 11 November 1991, 13 May 1993.

16. Urquidi interview.

17. *Idaho Statesman,* 10 May 1985.

18. Lemmon interview.

19. Jimmy Jausoro, interview by authors, 15 October 1991.

20. Ibid.

21. Lemmon interview.

22. Morrison Berriochoa, interview by authors, 21 April 1993.

23. Urquidi interview.

TWELVE. NEW RELATIONS

1. John Ysursa, interview by authors, 30 July 1993.

2. Ansotegui-Fereday Scholarship pamphlet.

3. Imanol Galdos, interview by authors, 23 June 1992.

4. Cecil Andrus, interview by authors, 30 July 1993.

5. President Ardanza's speech.

6. Adelia Garro, interview by authors, 25 May 1991; Basque Museum and Cultural Center Bylaws.

7. Dan Ansotegui, interview by authors, 11 March 1992.

8. *Boise City News,* 2 July 1937.

9. John Ysursa interview.

10. William A. Douglass and Jon Bilbao, *Amerikanuak: Basques in the New World* (Reno: University of Nevada Press, 1975), 317–18; *Idaho Free Press* and *Caldwell Tribune,* 21 May 1970.

11. Steve Achabal, interview by authors, 13 April 1990.

12. Dave Eiguren, interview by authors, 8 April 1993.

13. Gina Urquidi, interview by authors, 28 April 1993.

14. John Ysursa interview.

SELECTED BIBLIOGRAPHY

REFERENCES

Ada County Naturalization Records.

Alba, Richard D. *Ethnic Identity: The Transformation of White America.* New Haven: Yale University Press, 1990.

Alegria, Henry. *75 Years of Memoirs.* Caldwell, Idaho: Caxton Printers, 1981.

Alzola, Arsen."The Basque Experience." Murphy, Idaho: Owyhee County Historical Society, 1982.

Arrizabala, Luis. "Jaialdi '87 International Basque Festival Cultural Program Book."

Arrizabalaga, Marie Pierre. "A Statistical Study of Basque Immigration into California, Nevada, Idaho, and Wyoming, 1900–1910." Master's thesis, University of Nevada, Reno, September 1986.

Articles of Confederation of the American Basque Fraternity. 10 December 1928. Basque Museum and Cultural Center. Boise, Idaho.

Articles of Confederation of the Basque Museum and Cultural Center of Idaho, Inc. September 1985. Basque Museum and Cultural Center. Boise, Idaho.

Baker, Sarah Catherine. "Basque-American Folklore in Eastern Oregon." Master's thesis, University of California–Berkeley, 1972.

Bard, Rachel. "Aimery Picaud and the Basques: Selections from the Pilgrim's Guide to Santiago de Compostela." In *Essays in Basque Social Anthropology and History,* edited by William A. Douglass, 189–213. Reno: Basque Studies Program, University of Nevada, Reno, 1989.

Bender, Eugene I., and George Kagiwada. "Hansen's Law of 'Third Generation Return' and the Study of American Religio-Ethnic Groups." *Phylon* (1968): 360–70.

Berlin, Isaiah. "The Bent Twig: A Note on Nationalism." *Foreign Affairs* (1972): 11–30.

Bieter, Pat. "Basques in Idaho." Idaho Centennial Commission Issue.

———. "John Archabal and the American Basques." Unpublished paper, 1956.

———. "Letemendi's Boarding House." *Idaho Yesterdays* 37 (Spring 1993): 6–10.

———. "Reluctant Shepherds: The Basques in Idaho." *Idaho Yesterdays* 1, no. 2 (Summer 1957): 10–15.

Bilbao, Iban, and Chantel de Eguiluz. *Matrimonios Vascos en Idaho y Nevada (1862–1941).* Vitoria-Gasteiz, Spain: Diputación Foral de Alava, Consejo de Cultura, Seccion de Bibliografia y Diaspora Vasca, 1983.

————. *Vascos en el Censo de Población del Oeste Americano 1900.* Vitoria-Gasteiz, Spain: Diputación Foral de Alava, Consejo de Cultura, Seccion de Bibliografia y Diaspora Vasca, 1981.

Bilbao, Julio. "Basque Names in Early Idaho." *Idaho Yesterdays* 15 (Summer 1971): 26–29.

Bradley, Cyprian, and Edward J. Kelly. "History of the Diocese of Boise." Unpublished manuscript, 1942.

Brusen, Bernice. *Basques from the Pyrenees to the Rockies.* Portland: Dynagraphics, 1985.

Clark, Robert P. *The Basques: The Franco Years and Beyond.* Reno: University of Nevada Press, 1979.

Collins, Roger. *The Basques.* New York: Basil Blackwell, 1986.

Commonweal 39, 24 December 1943.

Congressional Record, 26 June 1964 and 30 December 1970.

Cressman, L. S., and Anthony Yturri. "The Basques in Oregon." *Commonwealth Review* (March 1938): 367–80.

Dinnerstein, Leonard, and David M. Reimers. *Ethnic Americans: A History of Immigration and Assimilation.* New York: Dodd, Mead, 1975.

Douglass, William A. "The Basques." In *Harvard Encyclopedia of American Ethnic Groups,* edited by Stephen Thernstrom. Cambridge: Harvard University Press, Belknap Press, 1980.

————. "The Basques of the American West: Preliminary Historical Perspectives." *Nevada Historical Quarterly* 13, no. 4 (Winter 1970): 12–25.

————. "Serving Girls and Sheepherders: Emigration and Continuity in a Spanish Basque Village." In *The Changing Faces of Rural Spain,* edited by Joseph B. Aceves and William A. Douglass, 45–61. New York: Schenkman Publishing, Halstead Press Division, John Wiley, 1976.

————. "The Vanishing Basque Sheepherder." *American West* 17 (July–August 1980): 30–31, 59–61.

Douglass, William A., and Jon Bilbao. *Amerikanuak: Basques in the New World.* Reno: University of Nevada Press, 1975.

Echevarria, Jeronima. "*Ostatuak Amerikanuak:* A History of Basque-American Boardinghouses." Ph.D. diss., University of North Texas, Denton, 1988.

Edlefsen, John B. "A Sociological Study of the Basques of Southwest Idaho." Ph.D. diss., State College of Washington, 1948.

Edmondson, Brad. "Making Yourself at Home: The Baby Boom Generation Yearns to Settle Down." *Utne Reader* (May/June 1990): 74–92.

Eiguren, Joe. *Kashpar.* Caldwell, Idaho: Caxton Printers, 1986.

Etulain, Richard W. "Basque Beginnings in the Pacific Northwest." *Idaho Yesterdays* 18, no. 1 (Spring 1974): 26–32.

Etulain, Richard W., and Jeronima Echeverria. *Portraits of Basques in the New World.* Reno: University of Nevada Press, 1999.

Euskalzaindia. *Bertsolari Txapelketa 1982.* Bilbao, Spain: Jagon-1, 1982.

Fishman, Joshua A. *The Rise and Fall of the Ethnic Revival: Perspectives on Language and Ethnicity.* New York: Mouton, 1965.

Gaiser, Joseph Harold. "The Basques of Jordan Valley: A Study of Social Process and Social Change." Ph.D. diss., University of Southern California, 1944.

Gallop, Rodney. *A Book of the Basques.* Reno: University of Nevada Press, 1970.

Gans, Herbert J. "Symbolic Ethnicity: The Future of Ethnic Groups and Cultures in America." *Ethnic and Racial Studies* (January 1979): 1–20.

Garatea, Paquita Lucia. "Burnseko Etxekoandreak: Basque Women Boarding House Keepers of Burns, Oregon." Master's thesis, Portland State University, 1990.

Gilfillan, Archer B. *Sheep.* Boston: Little, Brown, 1930.

Glazer, Nathan. *Ethnic Dilemmas.* Cambridge: Harvard University Press, 1983.

Glazer, Nathan, and Daniel P. Moynihan. "Why Ethnicity?" (October 1974): 33–39.

Gleason, Philip. "American Identity and Americanization." In *Harvard Encyclopedia of American Ethnic Groups,* edited by Stephen Thernstrom. Cambridge: Harvard University Press, Belknap Press, 1980.

Goering, John M. "The Emergence of Ethnic Interests: A Case of Serendipity." *Social Forces* (March 1971): 379–84.

Gordon, Milton. *Assimilation in American Life: The Role of Race, Religion, and National Origins.* New York: Oxford University Press, 1964.

Grant, Madison. *The Passing of the Great Race.* New York: Charles Scribner's Sons, 1916.

Gray, Margery P. "A Population and Family Study of Basques Living in Shoshone and Boise, Idaho." Ph.D. diss., University of Oregon, 1955.

Haddingham, Evan. "Europe's Mystery People." *World Monitor Magazine* 5 (September 1992): 34–42.

Handlin, Oscar, ed. *Children of the Uprooted.* New York: G. Braziller, 1966.

———. *The Uprooted.* Boston: Little, Brown, 1952.

Hanley, Mike, with Ellis Lucia. *Owyhee Trails: The West's Forgotten Corner.* Caldwell, Idaho: Caxton Printers, 1973.

Hansen, Marcus Lee. "The Third Generation: Search for Continuity." In *Children of the Uprooted,* edited by Oscar Handlin, 43–46. Englewood, N.J.: Prentice-Hall, 1959.

———. "The Third Generation: Search for Continuity." In *Social Perspectives on Behavior,* edited by H. D. Stein and R. A. Cloward. New York: Free Press, 1963.

Hart, Arthur. *Life in Old Boise.* Boise: Historic Idaho, Inc., and Boise City Celebrations, 1989.

Hawley, James H. *History of Idaho: The Gem of the Mountains.* Vol. 3. Chicago: Clarke Publishing, 1920.

Heiberg, Marianne. "Inside the Moral Community: Politics in a Basque Village." In *Basque Politics: A Case Study in Ethnic Nationalism,* edited by William A. Douglass. Reno: University of Nevada Press, 1985.

Herberg, Will. *Protestant, Catholic, Jew.* Garden City, N.Y.: Doubleday, 1955 and 1960.

Higham, John. *Strangers in the Land: Patterns of American Nativism, 1860–1925.* New Brunswick, N.J.: Rutgers University Press, 1955.

History of Idaho. Boise: C. J. Clarke Publishing, 1920.

Hooper, John. *The Spaniards: A Portrait of the New Spain.* Harmondsworth, Middlesex, England, and New York: Penguin Books, 1987.

Howe, Irving. *World of Our Fathers.* New York: Harcourt Brace Jovanovich, 1976.

Huxley-Barkham, Selma. *The Basque Coast of Newfoundland.* Plum Point, Newfoundland: Great Northern Peninsula Development Corporation, 1989.

Idaho Humanities Council and the Idaho Centennial Commission. "Women's Organizations in Idaho." 1990.

Idaho Wool Growers Bulletin. 14 February 1951, 30 January 1952.

Israelowitz, Oscar. *Ellis Island Guide.* Brooklyn, N.Y.: Israelowitz Publishing, 1990.

Keelan, Tom. "With the Miners Came the Sheep." *Boise Idaho Statesman Centennial Supplement,* 1990.

Kilher, Catherine A., and Charles P. Koch. *Sheep and Man.* Denver: American Sheep Producers Council, 1978.

Larrison, Earl J. *Owyhee: The Life of a Northern Desert.* Caldwell, Idaho: Caxton Printers, 1957.

Laxalt, Robert. "The Indomitable Basques." *National Geographic* (July 1985).

Lazerwitz, Bernard, and Louis Rowitz. "The Three Generations Hypothesis." *American Journal of Sociology* 69 (June 1964): 529–38.

Lescott-Leszcynski, John. *The History of U.S. Ethnic Policy and Its Impact on European Ethnics.* Boulder, Colo.: Westview, 1984.

Mathers, Michael. *Sheepherders: Men Alone.* Boston: Houghton Mifflin, 1975.

McCall, Grant E. "Basque-Americans and a Sequential Theory of Migration and Adaptation." Master's thesis, San Francisco State College, 1968.

McCullough, Sister Flavia Maria. "The Basques of the Northwest." Ph.D. diss., University of Portland, 1945.

Mindel, Charles H., and Robert W. Habenstein, eds. *Ethnic Families in America: Patterns and Variations.* New York: Elsevier, 1976.

Novak, Michael. *The Rise of the Unmeltable Ethnics.* New York: Macmillan, 1971.

Olsen, Evie. "Landas Tell of Sheepherding Days in Owyhees." *Owyhee (Idaho) Avalanche,* April 4, 1990.

La Organisación Independiente Sociale. Bylaws. 1933.

Payne, Stanley. *Basque Nationalism.* Reno: University of Nevada Press, 1975.

Petersen, William, Michael Novak, and Philip Gleason. *Concepts of Ethnicity.* Cambridge: Harvard University Press, Belknap Press, 1982.

Petrissans, Catherine M. "When Ethnic Groups Do Not Assimilate: The Case of Basque-American Resistance." *Ethnic Groups* 9 (1991): 61–81.

Podhoretz, Norman. *Making It.* New York: Random House, 1967.

Roesch, Ethel A. "Basques of the Sawtooth Range." *Frontier Times* (April–May 1964): 15.

San Sebastián, Koldo. *The Basque Archives: Vascos en Estados Unidos (1938–1943).* San Sebastián: Editorial Txertroa, n.d.

Sather, Clifford A. "Marriage Patterns Among the Basques of Shoshone." B.A. thesis, Reed College, 1961.

Scott, Franklin D. *The Peopling of America: Perspectives on Immigration.* Washington, D.C.: American Historical Association Pamphlets, 1963.

Shaddock, Louise. *Andy Little: Idaho Sheep King.* Caldwell, Idaho: Caxton Printers, 1990.

Sherlock, Patti. *Alone on the Mountain: Sheepherding in the American West.* Garden City, N.Y.: Doubleday, 1979.

"Shoshone and Idaho Perspectives." Booklet. Boise: Idaho Humanities Council, 1990.

Silen, Sol. *La historia de los Vascongados en el oeste de los Estados Unidos.* New York: Las Novedades, 1917.

Smith, Robert S. *Doctors and Patients.* Boise: Syms York, 1968.

Thursby, Jacqueline Schuster. "Basque Women in Caribou County." Master's thesis, Utah State University, 1991.

Urquidi, Richard. "History of the Mountain Home Basques." Master's thesis, Boise State University, 1980.

Waters, Mary C. *Ethnic Options: Choosing Identities in America.* Berkeley: University of California Press, 1990.

Wells, Merle. *Boise: An Illustrated History.* Woodland Hills, Calif.: Windsor Publications, 1982.

Wentworth, Edward. *America's Sheep Trails: History, Personalities.* Ames: Iowa State College Press, 1948.

Western Desert News Magazine (26 November 1950).

Yancey, William, Eugene P. Erickson, and Richard N. Juliani. "Emergent Ethnicity: A Review and Reformulation." *American Sociological Review.*

INTERVIEWS

Note: Conducted in Boise, Idaho, unless otherwise designated. Audiotapes may be found in the Basque Museum and Cultural Center.

Abraham, Julie. 25 March 1992.
Achabal, Dan. 2 August 1995.
Achabal, Simon. 13 May 1993.
Achabal, Steve. 13 April 1990.
Achabal, Toni. 22 March 1993 and 13 May 1993.
Alcelay, Jesus. 19 July 1993.
Aldape, Julie. 28 January 1992.
Aldecoa, Dorothy. 15 July 1996
Andrus, Cecil. 30 July 1993.
Anduiza, John. 21 March 1992.
Ansotegui, Dan. 11 March 1992.
Archabal, Marjorie. 19 June 1995.
Arguinchona, Laura. 10 March 1992.
Arrieta, Jose Luis. 23 February 1993.
Artiach, Jose Mari. 10 June 1993.
Artiach, Miren. 8 February 1992.
Aucutt, Sean. 18 July 1993.

Aucutt, Tom. 31 July 1993.

Barrinaga, Linda. 19 July 1993.

Bastida, John and Regina. 7 January 1992.

Beristain, Nick. 20 March 1992 and 7 June 1993.

Berriochoa, Morrison. 21 April 1993.

Bieter, Chris. 15 January 1992.

Bieter, Eloise. 12 February 1992.

Bieter, Pat. 10 March 1992 and 13 July 1993.

Bilbao, Amaya. 30 July 1993.

Bilbao, Anita. 12 July 1993.

Bilbao, Dan. 17 January 1992. Telephone call to San Francisco, California, from Boise, Idaho.

Bilbao, Frank and Frances. 9 February 1991. Cascade, Idaho.

Bilbao, Josie. 15 June 1993.

Bilbao, Julie. 23 June 1993.

Bilbao, Julio. 21 June 1993.

Bourgeaud, Olatz. 19 November 1992.

Cenarrusa, Pete. 9 June 1993.

Church, Bethine. 6 July 1993.

Clarkson, Cathy. 1 July 1993.

Dick, Rosie. 20 February 1992.

Douglass, William A. 4 August 1993. Reno, Nevada.

Echevarria, Ray. 20 March 1992.

Eiguren, Dave. 8 April 1993.

Eiguren, Fred and Isabel. 20 February 1991.

Eiguren, Joe. 4 December 1991, 18 February 1992, and 24 March 1993.

Erquiaga, Albert. 11 November 1991 and 13 May 1993.

Galdos, Imanol. 23 June 1992.

Garatea, Lucy. 7 February 1992.

Garmendia, Virginia. 22 August 1993.

Garro, Adelia. 25 May 1991.

Hormaechea, Juanita. 28 September 1991 and 6 July 1993.

Jausoro, Jimmy. 15 October 1991.

Lachiondo, Lydia. 19 July 1992.

Landa, Sabino. 18 March 1992.

Laradogoitia, Antone. 10 February 1991.

Larrinaga, Angela. 4 September 1993.

Lawson, Toni. 24 July 1993.

Lemmon, Ron. 15 March 1992.

Lotina, Ray. 16 February 1991.

Malone, Jeremy. 25 April 1993.

Mendiola, Anes. 13 February 1992.

Mendive, Steve. 29 June 1993.

Miller, Patty. 1 July 1993.

Peplinski, Father. 19 March 1992.

Perry-Bauer, Barbara. 17 April 1992.

Sarria, Justo. 10 March 1992.

Seielstad, Andrea and Mark. 2 June 1993.

Uriarte, Marie. 14 July 1993.

Urquidi, Gina. 28 April 1993.

Walsh, Nicholas. 13 January 1992. Telephone call to Twin Falls, Idaho, from Boise, Idaho.

Yribar, Stack. 2 February 1992.

Ysursa, Asuncion. 18 March 1992.

Ysursa, John. 30 July 1993.

Ysursa, Ray. 15 July 1996.

Zabala, Lino. 5 June 1993.

INDEX